meDItatION
for everyday living

meditation

for everyday living

STEPHEN AUSTEN

 A GODSFIELD BOOK

Dedication
For my beloved wife Carla, whose love and
support provided the inspiration for this book.

First published in Great Britain in 2002
by Godsfield Press Ltd
Laurel House, Station Approach, Alresford
Hampshire SO24 9JH, U.K.

10 9 8 7 6 5 4 3

Designed for Godsfield Press by
The Bridgewater Book Company

Photography by Walter Gardiner
Picture Research by Lynda Marshall

Printed and bound in China

ISBN 1-84181-148-3

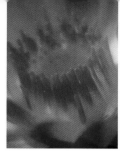

contents

preface

I first began to practice meditation when I was 16 years old.
There were many reasons why someone so young should choose
this. First, I suppose I was somewhat unusual in that I had very
early spiritual experiences. I tried to find answers to the deeper
questions of life in conventional religion, but I did not find the
practical guidance I longed for. I knew that I needed an "inner"
connection, so, unaided (and without the availability of good books
on the subject) I began to meditate alone. What consequently
transpired over the weeks, months, and years from that first
moment that I sat and "went within" has transformed my life.
I am not superhuman, yet through meditative states I have
benefited from many incredible experiences. Many of these
experiences are not easy to describe, but I can say that I have
found my inner Self there, that all-pervading Self that transcends
the lesser, personality "I." In those blissful moments of inner peace,
I have heard the "still, small voice" of intuition and have touched
the beating heart of the Universe. Only in meditation
have I ever experienced the "peace that passes all understanding"
of which so many mystics down the ages have spoken.

There is a very great need in all of us to find an inner peace and
stillness. Largely speaking, religion has failed to fill the spiritual void
that has been generated by the swamp of materialism, and we feel

engulfed by the pressures of an ever more demanding society. The world seems to be a very uncertain, confusing, and frightening place to be living in. But in meditation we gain clarity and insight into why things are as they appear. We learn to understand ourselves and the world more clearly and see beneath the surface. Our mindset changes perspective, and thus we are enabled to cope with the troubles that are thrown upon us and maybe even transform our lives completely. By creating a daily discipline to reconnect to your true Self, you will be fulfilling your needs for inner peace, harmony, and stillness. I understand your need for inner peace amid the storms of life, for I have also walked that same road with you. I am here to assist you on your journey through the exercises on the accompanying CD.

I have worked in several fields of experience, variously employed as a screenprinter for many years, a lifeguard and swimming instructor, artist, laborer, film extra, and model. In 1984 at the age of 23, I believe I was the youngest Full Healer Member of the National Federation of Spiritual Healers (NFSH) in Great Britain. I now live in Calgary, Canada, with my wife Carla. My work currently involves healing, teaching, counseling, mediumship, channeling, meditation instruction, and writing—all with the hope of inspiring others to travel the path to their own inner happiness.

1: what is meditation?

What is meditation? This question has been asked by countless generations stretching back through the centuries. Describing the process of meditation is no easy task; it daunted me when I first thought of writing this book. Yet, because the benefits of meditation are so enormous and far-reaching, I felt compelled to share with others my knowledge which is based on more than twenty years' experience of this incredible self-help technique.

Meditation has so many benefits that it is impossible to compile a complete list of them. These benefits range from the purely physical, such as reduced pulse rate, better sleep patterns, healthier skin, and a delaying of the aging process, to the emotional, such as greater control over the emotions themselves, handling and getting in touch with your deeper feelings in a more positive way, and reducing or even eliminating negative emotional states such as anger, mood-swings, grief, guilt, embarrassment,

and low self-esteem. Meditation brings greater peace of mind, increases the capacity to handle stress, enhances willpower and the capacity to deal with heavy mental workloads. Meditation also has great spiritual benefits. For those who have spiritual leanings, either in a religious sense or in a wider context, meditation is an essential part of spiritual evolution. Your connection to that Greater Power (or whichever name you choose to give it) will be vastly enhanced by going inward and meditating. Meditation is an exploration of the inner Self. But describing that process can be difficult. The meditator is like an experienced caver who has returned from discovering a magnificently beautiful cave that is full of precious jewels.

The caver excitedly begins to tell his friends what he has found, and as much as they can clearly see that he has undergone a wonderful experience, they cannot actually appreciate what he has discovered. No matter how much he tells his audience that they too must come and see this glorious cave full of precious stones, glittering pools, and multicolored rock formations, they are wary and hold back from venturing into some dark unknown place deep within the bowels of the Earth, and even begin to claim that the excitable caver is exaggerating or deluded. Entering into the Self can be likened to descending into a very deep cave, and many are fearful of such unknown territory. "Why should we go into this cave?" the friends protest. "It is safe here on the surface with things we know and trust."

But the caver knows that when equipped with appropriate tools there is nothing to fear. Those who are fearful of the depths of the Self—and are afraid to venture into the cave—do not know how to equip themselves for the journey and will therefore never experience the bliss that resides in the innermost Self.

In this book, I will provide you with all the necessary equipment needed to venture into the cave of the Self. Rest assured that there really is nothing to fear. Fear arises only because of inaccurate preconceptions and lack of experience. If you follow the guidelines set out in this book, you will gain in personal experience and will be able to cast off all doubts and fears.

To explain a little more about meditation, I should perhaps outline what meditation is *not*. Meditation is not a process whereby you enter into a sleep condition. Far from falling asleep or becoming unconscious, your mental acuity is actually improved. There is a clarity, a sharpness to the mind that rarely exists in ordinary everyday consciousness. You will find that your awareness of bodily functions increases; for example, you may be aware of your heart beating while in meditation, which, although a little unnerving at first, will soon pass. You will be conscious of how the breath flows in and out of the lungs and how the body sits when in repose. You may seem to itch and feel a need to stretch or move around until comfortable.

All of these minor sensitivities are natural at first, but after regular practice they will pass. You will also become aware of how you feel emotionally, and often negative feelings, such as doubt, fear, worries, sorrow, and anger, will rise to the surface of the mind, so much so that you may say to yourself, "I've had enough of this meditation game; it's making me miserable." But if you persevere, the negative states dissolve away and you will gradually enter into a peaceful condition. The process of sitting for meditation at first highlights all the negativity that currently exists within your own

emotional and mental makeup, but if you are prepared to work through it, like the courageous cave explorer who overcomes the potholes and rocks in his path, the rewards of your efforts will far outweigh the initial difficulties—I promise you.

Some Christians may feel that meditation belongs to Eastern religions and therefore has no place in Christian practice. This is not true. Meditation is not something that should be feared as being somehow pagan or non-Christian, and in fact has been practiced by many famous Christian saints such as St. Augustine and St. Francis of Assisi. Meditation formed part of the early Christian Church, as far back as its founder Jesus Christ and his immediate disciples. Prior to this, the Old Testament prophets and seers of Judaism practiced meditation regularly, and there is even an account in Genesis of Isaac meditating in a field. King David refers to his meditations throughout the Psalms, and his son Solomon was renowned for his wisdom as a result of his meditative nature.

Meditation is not the province of any particular religious ideology. I believe that you can meditate quite effectively even if you have no belief in any God whatsoever or in any afterlife, for meditation is a state of mind rather than a religious practice.

However, if the individual does have some kind of religious leaning or, better still, a broader, more all-embracing spiritual concept of life, then meditation can be a deeper, richer experience than if it is practiced as a purely mechanical technique. When meditation is grounded in a feeling of love, devotion, or aspiration toward some deity or greater being, it will have more profound effects than when it is based on a nondevotional approach.

Nevertheless, readers should not feel that I am encouraging them to join some religious organization. I do not belong to any religious group myself. I must emphasize that a particular religious persuasion is not necessary, and in fact, in certain cases, approaching meditation with a limited frame of mind based on a particular religious angle can be most undesirable. It is better by far if the meditator has an open attitude concerning God, or a supreme being, life after death, and life's purpose. A positive and open-minded attitude enables the meditator to experience the depths of meditation in all its beauty without restrictive, negative mental and emotional blocks that hinder spiritual evolution. For meditation is nothing if not the individual actively taking part in the *conscious* direction of his or her own evolution.

This evolution can only proceed through developing the emotions and the mind, to the point where you are no longer a slave to either of them. If you control the mind and the emotions, even the body will fall into line with this new way of being. Far-fetched? Not so.

Roger Bannister, who in 1954 was the first man to run a mile in under four minutes, claimed that his achievement

relied not only on his physical training but also on his mental power. It takes mental determination to achieve such a feat, because the power of the mind is greater than that of the physical body. Another athlete who believed in the power of mental focusing is Linford Christie. Prior to a race he would stand at the end of the 100-meter track staring ahead to the finish line. Christie developed a "tunnel vision" approach that blocked out all other thoughts and focused his mind solely on reaching the finish line before anyone else. His achievements depended on far more than his physical athleticism.

Meditation develops the same kind of tunnel vision approach—a technique whereby the mind is focused on just one thought, one idea. It is this type of focusing that helps you to achieve your goals. It is more commonly known as *concentration*.

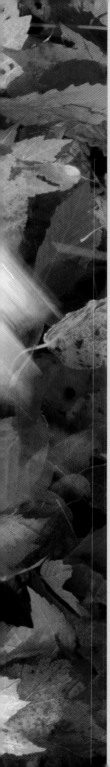

CONCENTRATION

Before you can even hope to meditate properly, you must first develop the ability to concentrate. Now this may seem a challenging prospect. But you do it all the time, for instance, when you are driving, especially if you are driving around an unfamiliar area, while trying to read a map to find your way. The person who works at a precision machine, crafting tools to a specified size, must concentrate for many hours. Playing tennis requires concentration to watch the other player's moves; painting a house or a portrait is impossible without concentration; even reading a novel or watching a movie requires concentration in order to follow the plot. All of us concentrate in innumerable ways that perhaps we do not usually consider. Even mundane chores such as mowing the lawn or cleaning the house require a certain amount of concentration if they are to be done well and efficiently.

Concentration comes in varying degrees of intensity. It may be that certain mundane tasks do not require a great deal of concentration, while other, more specialized skills require very intense concentration indeed. While performing a boring household chore, your mind may wander, or be half alert to what is on the radio, for example, and you think that the task is still done satisfactorily. Perhaps it is, but I would suggest that if any task is given full attention from the mind without any distractions, then the job is probably completed in half the time, because the mental processes are fully attentive. Consider for example someone reading a novel while the television is blaring in the background. The television constantly interrupts the free flow of thought, causing the reader to become stuck on the same sentence, constantly trying to pick up the threads of the novel. Before long, the plot is lost. Clearly, it would be best to switch the television off. But with proper training in concentration an experienced meditator can read with a focused mind while the television is on and other people in the room are engaged in conversation. She has learned to shut out the distraction.

Meditation itself is not possible without concentration. In this book, as well as on the accompanying CD, I will guide you on your journey to reach the depths of the meditative experience. I will be like the caver leading the novice into the bowels of the Earth. One of the tools I shall give you is the ability to improve your concentration. Try to regard concentration as the grappling hook that you can use to fix yourself upon a single thought and thus anchor your mind securely while you explore the inner world.

I will give you one more example of concentration so that you may have a clearer picture of the process that leads to meditation. In the early days of my working life, at the age of just 17, I trained as a silkscreen printer. One of the tasks I was given, being a trainee, was to mix up the pigments for the printing inks. At first I saw this task as a boring job and I did it reluctantly. To make the ink, I had to scoop out the pigment with a spatula and mix it with two gooey substances, and pour it all into a small grinding machine. I then sat in front of the machine watching the mixture churn, run through the grinder, and flow into a container. It was a boring job. Nevertheless, it was not long before I became fascinated by the process, staring at the colored pigment and observing it swirl and spiral into the grinding machine. After several minutes had passed, lulled by the soft, monotonous sound of the grinder and mesmerized by the swirling ink mixture, which often made attractive patterns, I noticed that my boredom had vanished and that I had instead become spellbound. My mind had shut out all other thoughts, and I was completely mentally focused on my task. Whenever I mixed pigments after that, I found that I looked forward to the job, and before long, I entered a deeply concentrated state akin to meditation. Yet my mind was not dulled, and neither did this place me in any danger, either from any equipment or from drowsiness. My mind was in fact sharper and more alert. I had by this time in my life already discovered meditation, and this simple task improved my meditation practice, which I continued at home. I had learned something valuable from this experience—*concentration leads to meditation.*

2: first steps

So how do we train the mind to concentrate? There are many methods, but two of the best that I know are "breath counting" and "candle gazing."

BREATH COUNTING

Seat yourself in a comfortable position that suits you, and in which you can remain for 15 minutes. If you are experienced in Yoga, you may wish to sit in the Half Lotus or Lotus (see figures 1 and 2), but most people will prefer to sit in a comfortable armchair or a firm-backed chair. Set an alarm clock for 15 minutes, taking care to use a gentle-sounding alarm that will not startle you. Now, close your eyes and begin to feel the free flow of your breath. The breath should come in through the nostrils and back out through the nostrils. You will find that this method of breathing will be the most beneficial for inducing a relaxed, meditative state. Mouth breathing does not give you this. The technique is easy; you count on every out-breath. So, for the first out-breath, you mentally count "One," then for the second, count "Two," for the third, count "Three," and for the fourth, count "Four." Remember that all counting is done mentally, not verbally. The goal is to keep the mind focused on the counting. Then, begin the cycle again, counting the first out-breath and so on up to the fourth breath. Continue in this manner until your alarm terminates this practice in concentration.

1 Half Lotus In this cross-legged position only one foot is placed upon the opposite thigh.

2 Lotus In the full Lotus both feet are placed on the thighs. These poses provide support for the trunk to rest in an upright position.

Remember also that, at this stage, this practice is still a concentration exercise and not proper meditation. All you are aiming to achieve in this practice is to continue steadily counting the out-breaths so that the mind remains concentrated on one line of thought. It is inevitable that other, unwanted thoughts will interrupt your practice,

and this is where you will encounter your first test in concentration. Your task now is to eliminate these other invading thoughts by using your willpower. You may wish to use the breath-counting exercise on the CD, which also includes a timed sequence.

Everyone has willpower, and it can be used to great personal advantage. Even if you think that your willpower is weak, you are in fact in possession of great willpower in more ways than you are aware of currently. The breath counting techniques, like so many others that you will be learning from this book, will draw out your latent willpower, dust if off, and get it functioning effectively once more. So, during your breath-counting exercise, as soon as the unwanted thoughts start to invade and annoy you, bring the mind back and focus on the act of counting. That's all you need to do, and this very constancy of thought is an act of the will.

After the 15 minutes are up, you may feel slightly mentally drained or, on the other hand, you may feel exhilarated. Most people find that the 15 minutes pass very quickly and enjoyably. It may be that, to start with, you hate doing the breath counting, but if you practice regularly every day, you will eventually come to enjoy the exercise. Gradually, you will find that your mind has become steadier and more focused, and that you can concentrate more easily on other things as well as the breath counting; you will consequently feel more relaxed, less tense, less fatigued, and more mentally peaceful as you go about your everyday life.

CANDLE GAZING

Candle gazing takes our practice of concentration one step
farther. This time, choose a candle that you find pleasing to the
eye and put it in a candleholder or on a candlestick. Place the
candle in its holder on an empty table free of clutter, directly in
front of you, and seat yourself before it on a comfortable chair
with a straight back. Light the candle and position it so that the
flame is as close to eye level as possible. Darken the room by
turning off the lights and closing the drapes. Obviously, make
sure that there is nothing flammable nearby, and that the candle
is firmly secured and cannot fall over. Set your soft-toned alarm
clock for just 5 minutes (you may increase this time by up to 15
minutes once you have become a very experienced candle gazer)
and insure that your sitting position feels comfortable for the
duration. The distance between the eyes and the candle should
be no more than about two feet, and no closer than about one
foot. Now, to begin. Use the breathing technique you learned
from breath counting, only this time do not count the breaths,
just allow the in-breath and out-breath to flow in a steady, slow,
deep, and relaxed manner. Gaze softly at the candle flame. Allow
the eyes to feel soft, not hard or staring. In this exercise all you
are doing is simply observing the play of the candle flame as it
burns on the wick. Begin to feel that, as you breathe, you are
being drawn into the flame mentally, that is, your eyes are
becoming gradually more attentive to the flame. Slowly, as you
use the constant, rhythmic breathing to keep the mind and the
eyes focused gently upon the flame, you will find yourself
becoming fascinated by the glowing flame in front of you, as it
moves slightly in little eddies on the wick.

Keep your eyes on one point of the flame as much as possible, perhaps upon the glowing white tip or the yellow flame lower down or the bluish flame where it burns on the wick itself. Here comes the testing part: you must not move your eyes, either to the left or right, or up or down, and you must not let them flick away to glance at any other objects in the room or look behind the candle in the distance. You must hold your attention on the flame—only the flame—not the body of the candle or the candlestick. Holding your gaze steady, with soft eyes and regular breathing, try not to blink. If you must there should be long intervals in between each blink. This is virtually impossible for many people, and everyone finds this part of the practice difficult at first. But, with continuous, regular practice, even the need to blink will naturally subside as you are drawn deeper into the experience. The candle-gazing experience can be really quite meditative, even though it is primarily a practice in concentration rather than actual meditation.

With softly focused eyes and regular breathing, the five minutes will pass very rapidly, and you will undoubtedly want to extend this delightful practice in concentration. Immediately after your alarm has informed you that the session is over, try one more pleasurable thing: gently place the palms of your hands over your closed eyes (taking care not to press the palms onto the eyeballs) and watch for the afterimage of the candle to appear in your mind's eye. Assuming that the room was dark enough and you followed the practice correctly, the afterimage of the candle will have registered on the retina at the back of the eyes. You will see an image of a bright yellow flame that looks exactly like the actual flame. Now watch what happens. The afterimage will begin to glow through a wonderful kaleidoscope of beautiful and fascinating colors. You will see red, orange, green, blue, indigo, and violet, as well as the original yellow— all the colors of the spectrum—brighter and more vivid than anything you have seen before. Enjoy this moment.

What has happened is that the color-sensitive cells in the retina of the eyes, known as cone cells, have registered the colors inherent in the candle flame and recorded them on the retina walls. Gradually the colors will fade, and you will be left with a soothing black void, which in itself is pleasant. When you feel ready, you can put the lights back on, blow out your candle, and assimilate what has happened to you.

So, what has happened to you? Didn't your mind enjoy five minutes or so of focused attention upon *one object* (the flame) and didn't your breathing become slower and steadier? Didn't you find that unwanted thoughts couldn't grab your attention, because your mind was pinpointed on one spot? Then, when you closed your eyes and looked inward at the mental image of the flame, you took the process a little farther, and still the unwanted thoughts didn't come in and distract your attention. Something wonderful had happened. First, your eyes were completely focused on one thing; second, your breath assisted you in staying focused; and third, you were then able to focus inwardly on the mind's eye. But best of all, the unwanted, irritating, distracting, nagging thoughts didn't bother you. What a freedom that is!

Assimilate what candle gazing has taught you. You were able to focus outwardly in a very different way than you have been used to, and in a most agreeable way as well. Then you took this a step farther by focusing inwardly as well, an exercise that perhaps you didn't think was possible for you. But you did it. I didn't do it for you; all I did was guide you. *You* did it. Well done.

It is a good idea to practice your breath counting regularly, and particularly the candle gazing, while still in the process of learning from this book and CD. A regular, daily practice will prepare your mind and train it. A good gardener fertilizes the soil before planting the seeds that will produce the flowers. In these exercises we are like the attentive gardener, fertilizing the soil of the mind in order to promote a flowering forth during the practice of meditation. A good regime might be to do breath counting every morning for 15 minutes and candle gazing every evening for at least 5 minutes, extending up to 15 minutes.

If you now accept that concentration, even concentrating inwardly in the mind, is possible for you, then meditation itself and all its manifold benefits will soon follow.

3: bubbling thoughts

In the preceding chapter I gave you the necessary tools to make a beginning: breath counting and candle gazing. Breath counting showed you that the mind and the breath are interrelated, that one inevitably affects the other. This is important information, and if you continue to use the breath to steady the mind, this technique will stand you in good stead throughout your journey in the meditation experience.

In terms of the analogy of the caver, the breath might represent the caving rope attached to the grappling hook of the mind. As the mind draws you along the sometimes difficult pathways of the inner world, the breath keeps you fixed upon the goal of finding the treasures that are hidden deep within the cave.

The experiment in candle gazing showed you the link between the mind and the breath more directly and objectively, and you also learned that consciously controlling the breath could help you to concentrate upon just one object. Even with the eyes closed, and inwardly focusing the mind upon the candle's afterimage, the breath held the mind in concentrated attention, even if by now the breathing had slowed down to a minimum. In our cave analogy, candle gazing is the lantern that lights your way.

Truly, candle gazing is a point of focus for the mind and a practice that sheds much "light" on the process of concentration and how to improve it. In chapter 1 I gave some brief examples to explain the essential character of concentration and how it is actually second nature to all of us. Let us now extend our understanding of concentration a little farther.

CONCENTRATION AND THOUGHT CONTROL

The first task in improving concentration is learning to control the constant bubbling of the thought waves. The mind is always restless in those who have little or no experience of meditation. It is important to gain control over unwanted thoughts such as worries, petty annoyances, fears, and hatreds. You are already learning to control these bubbling thoughts during the practice of breath counting and candle gazing, but this control may not extend into your everyday life. But if you can manage to regulate these unwanted thoughts during daily experience, and thereby focus the mind on *one thought* rather than

on a whole host of scattered throughts, then in time you will attain mental peace and equilibrium. This peace then develops into the bliss state spoken of by many mystics through the centuries. And from personal experience I can assure you that the bliss state is worth working toward, even if it takes a long, long time to achieve.

How then, do you gain mastery over these unwanted thoughts? Do you attempt to struggle with them and thus conquer them? No. This approach is always counterproductive and actually reinforces the negative state of the thought waves. The secret of

controlling unwanted dominating thoughts is not to give them any attention; the unwanted thoughts die out by themselves. By not feeding these thoughts with your mental energy, they fade out through lack of mental stimulation and become starved of energy.

In our caving analogy, these unwanted thought waves are the distorted shadows thrown onto the rough cave walls, roof, and floor—distortions that are often seemingly made worse by the light from your lantern, that is, the light of your own wiser, higher mind. You see, as the mind becomes more focused through the practice of breath-counting and candle-gazing exercises, the unwanted thoughts seem to come up with redoubled force. This is because the contrast between your stilled mind and your usual restless thoughts makes the negative mental waves appear worse than before.

In time, though, the undesirable thoughts will become less potent, and you will derive great pleasure from this. Do not give up your practice in breath counting and candle gazing simply because you might find the discipline tedious. Millions of people use the gym to keep physically fit even though they do not see any results until several weeks have passed. But they know that persistence pays off, and the results are worth the initial difficulties in gaining the necessary discipline.

Breath counting and candle gazing should be treated as exercises to train the mind for meditation. Only discipline and a firm commitment to practice regularly will insure success. You will be glad that you stuck with it.

One important thing to remember about concentration practices is that they should not be confined only to the 15 minutes of breath counting or the 5 minutes or so of candle gazing; rather they should be connected to your daily routines. You should look forward to them as pleasurable experiences and not duties that you want to hurry up and finish so that you can get on with other things. When you return to ordinary life after your practices, do not immediately rush up and charge headlong into your duties, but sit awhile and assimilate what you have gained from the experience.

Then, when you return to other affairs, try to maintain the same sense of peace in your everyday activities as you have enjoyed during the breath counting or candle gazing. The secret of these exercises is gradually to extend the experience gained from them into everyday life. Instead of spending a wonderful 5 to 15 minutes of focused attention on the candle flame only to jump up and ruin the practice by trying to sort out a million tasks, take a few moments to assimilate the experience after closing your eyes. When you open them again, try to hold the inner mental focus in a relaxed and peaceful way and apply that to all other tasks, dealing with one thing at a time. This cultivates patience, and you will find that each task will be completed more efficiently than it would have been in an agitated state of mind.

For example, if after breath counting you must drive somewhere, continue to breathe in a regular, relaxed manner, not counting the breaths anymore (and obviously with your eyes open!) but feeling that the breathing continues its smooth, even, relaxed flow while you carry out the maneuvers of changing gear, indicating, steering, etc. You will discover that the whole driving experience is much more pleasurable, far less stressful, and that you reach your destination in a relaxed, peaceful frame of mind.

THE BENEFITS OF A CONCENTRATED MIND

By extending the effects of breath counting and candle gazing, you heighten your powers of concentration, and everything you do, from basic household chores to complicated technical work, is completed more satisfactorily and enjoyably than before. With a concentrated mind all your duties are completed in a shorter space of time and yet not in a hurried, rushed manner. When operating with complete mental attention, you will find that the whole process has speeded up by degrees. You make fewer mistakes, do not have mishaps, and are not easily distracted. You will notice another very important benefit: the unwanted, niggling thoughts are becoming shut out and eliminated. The mind is free to concentrate on the job at hand, and such freedom generates greater mental power. It is erroneous to think that a busy mind is a powerful mind. It is the still, silent mind that has power. You will learn more about this later. Store this information away for now and ponder it.

Another beneficial side effect of your concentration practices is that your memory will improve. Why does this happen? Because a mind that has become truly focused

fully records all the details of everything that happens. If you are watching a movie, for instance, but thinking about something else, you may miss vital parts of the plot; and likewise, if someone is talking to you but your mind is elsewhere, you may not actually hear what the person is saying, perhaps losing important points of the discourse. But with the development of an attentive, uncluttered mind, you will slowly become aware that your memory for details has improved vastly, and a good memory can only enhance any individual's life.

DEALING WITH NEGATIVE THOUGHTS

Having ventured into the realms of the thought-world, you have learned
something about the nature of your own mind. You have no doubt discovered that
the constant stream of unnecessary thoughts is often quite out of control, and that
whenever you practice breath counting or candle gazing these unwanted thoughts
continue to surface and attempt to interrupt the smooth flow of your concentration.

You have probably already experienced for yourself the futility of trying to stem the flow of these thoughts by somehow combating them with an act of will; no matter how hard you try to blot out these thoughts or cease their flow, they only seem to come on with redoubled force. But by now, with continued practice of your two concentration exercises, you will have realized that the only way to gain freedom from these bubbling thought waves is by focusing on something else—that is, your own breathing or the candle flame. However, you cannot of course be watching your breath or gazing at the flame of a candle at all times of the day, so how else can you separate yourself from the unwanted thought processes?

During daily life, the best method of eliminating these thoughts is by refusing to participate in the games the mind plays. In other words, as unwanted mental impressions arise, such as fear, anger, resentment, grief, loss, and envy, the secret is not to allow the mind to dwell on these thought waves. Let them go. As a negative thought comes in, say, arising out of feelings of rejection, merely observe the thought, learn anything that you must from it, and then refuse to dwell upon it. Let the thought "I have been rejected" pass away. If other thoughts come in, reinforcing the initial thought with mental statements such as "I'm sick of being rejected all the time," and you slowly feel yourself being sucked into a negative spiral, try to replace this thought with something positive, perhaps the opposite of rejection. Think of all those times, no matter how small, when you were not rejected, but were praised and accepted. Replacing negative thoughts with positive thoughts often helps to eliminate the disturbing mental vibrations. Failing this, the wisest choice is simply to let the thought go and refuse to play the game. I say "simply," and I can hear you protesting that it is not so simple, but virtually impossible! But, with training, it can be done, which is why I am giving you exercises such as breath counting and candle gazing. With regular practice in these two exercises alone, your thoughts will become more stilled, less anxious, and uncluttered. It is up to you. If you undertake regular, disciplined practice every day, you will take great strides toward gaining peace of mind and will thus be nearer to entering the threshold of meditation itself.

Later I will show you how to meditate upon your emotions, which will assist you further in eliminating unwanted states of mind and feelings. But for now, use your breath as a tool for eradicating the negative thoughts. If you are suddenly assailed by a torrent of mental negativity, take some time away from your daily dealings (just a few minutes will usually suffice) and do some steady breath counting in order to rebalance yourself. The mind and breath are interwoven. The one affects the other. The breath is a powerful tool, so use it to help you in your quest for inner peace.

4: DRAWING BREATH

In this chapter, I will continue the discussion of the breath and how it affects your body, emotions, and mind. But first it will be useful to have a brief review of the mechanism of breathing and its physiological processes.

RESPIRATION

When we breathe in, the air is sucked into the trachea, the main tube that leads directly to both of the lungs. The trachea divides into two separate airways, each one serving one of the two lungs. The air passes through these tubes and enters the bronchi, the airways that pass directly into the lungs themselves. The bronchi are further subdivided into bronchioles, which are increasingly smaller airways, and these deliver the inspired air into the little air sacs of the lungs known as alveoli.

Now the magic happens. The alveoli are completely surrounded by an extensive network of minute blood vessels, the capillaries. Oxygen transfer takes place here very rapidly. It happens like this: as soon as the air enters the alveoli (which are in

direct contact with the blood capillaries) the oxygen content in the inspired air is immediately absorbed by the red blood cells and transported at lightning speed into the bloodstream. At the same time the red blood cells give up the load of carbon dioxide— the waste product of cell metabolism— that they are carrying away from the various parts of the body.

The alveoli accept this waste carbon dioxide in return for giving oxygen, and hence you breathe out this waste material into the atmosphere, where it is reabsorbed by trees and other vegetation. So there is a constant recycling of the air we inspire and expire. Nothing is wasted, and nothing is destroyed; it merely changes its state. The components of the air we breathe have actually been in existence for countless millennia, constantly altering from one state of being into another. It is a sobering and awe-inspiring thought that you are breathing the very same components of air breathed in by ancient peoples, including well-known historical figures. Any one of us could be breathing in the same atoms of air that Julius Caesar once breathed! It is part of a natural cycle as ageless as the tides that have ebbed and flowed far longer than humankind can recall.

Think about what all the billions of blood cells in your body must be doing. They are carrying life-giving energy in the form of oxygen molecules throughout the body and delivering their precious load to all the cells in the body. That means that all the internal and external organs are nourished with oxygen. No bodily metabolism (the process whereby the cells bring about the necessary chemical reactions that promote growth, production of energy, and elimination of waste) is possible without the presence of oxygen. Oxygen is the primary chemical that makes the bodily factory tick over—it is the essence of life itself.

Therefore, a simple intake of breath is an incredible event, one that starts up a huge chemical chain reaction at the cellular level throughout the physical body. Your body. Your breath. Breath circulates throughout the body; it even enters the nervous system and the brain. What can this mean for the meditative process? It means that the breath has great influence, that it affects all quarters, even that place where thoughts arise in the first place. This is highly significant. Without oxygen the brain cells die very quickly, but with a healthy flow of regular oxygen, the brain cells are stimulated to perform all their normal functions. And those functions are enhanced if the breath is channeled *consciously.*

But what are we talking about here? Am I saying that by doing a few breathing exercises you will gain a more alert mind? In one sense, yes, but it's much more than that. The act of breathing is not just a case of the cells being oxygenated so that the metabolism functions more efficiently, because breathing is not merely a physical act confined to bodily activities. Correct breathing, or *pranayama*, as it will be called from now on, is a means by which spiritual energy is stimulated and circulated throughout the body, which in turn affects the emotions and the mind.

PRANAYAMA

The term pranayama is a Sanskrit word derived from two words. The first word, *prana*, refers to the energy contained within the breath, which is composed of

millions of particles or globules that attach themselves to oxygen molecules and pervade the atmosphere around us. Prana is also known in Chinese mysticism as *chi*, the chi force or chi energy. Tai Chi is a whole science of movements dedicated to harnessing this chi force and utilizing it for physical, emotional, and mental health, poise, and control. Prana and chi are synonymous terms. Prana itself has not yet been recognized by modern science and remains a theory confined to the realms of mysticism, but those who use their prana wisely know the truth of its existence. It can be felt and experienced if not actually measured by any scientific instruments. Before you reject the idea of an invisible, mystical force called prana, remember that it was not so long ago that people could not measure or examine oxygen molecules. All we knew was that somehow we breathed in an invisible gas without which we would die. Yet even though the gas we now know as oxygen had not yet been identified or even proven to exist, no one denied that an undiscovered force sustained our lives and had always sustained us since the time that humans first drew breath. Prana is the life force par excellence, and I predict that one day in the not too distant future, humankind will discover its presence and be able to measure it scientifically. But until that day comes, you, the reader, will have to trust me.

The second part of the word pranayama, *yama*, refers to a discipline, spiritual practice, or purification technique. Therefore, pranayama means a disciplined technique of breath control; more specifically, pranayama means directing prana to various locations in the body and channeling it consciously in order to purify, cleanse, empower, and uplift.

During the practice of breath counting, which you are hopefully doing regularly, prana can be used to alter your current perceptions or perspectives. The aim is to channel prana so that negative vibrations found in the emotions and the mind can be steadily, slowly, and safely eliminated. I emphasize safely, for the methods I will show you will not harm you and are not to be used in any forced way. The whole process is gradual, but this is most effective because the process has a cumulative value. Doing a little pranayama whenever you feel like it and then dropping it through boredom or laziness will not help you; you will not see the results or recognize the value of the practice. But regular practice every day over several weeks and months will bring many beneficial results, and you will discover that your efforts are worthwhile.

Before I give you some pranayama techniques to try for yourself, let us first discover a little more about prana, or pranic energy.

An exact physiological description is not possible yet, for no scientific instrument has been invented that can analyze the structure of prana or even prove its existence. Instead, we have to rely on mystic teachings of the past and our own direct personal experience. What we do know about prana is that this mystical energy is the basic life force of the entire universe and the planet upon which we all live; all the Earth's myriad life forms—animal, vegetable, and mineral—exist because of prana. Prana fills all things. Nothing can exist without prana, not even so-called inanimate objects such as the table and chair I am writing at, or the chair you are sitting on, or this very book in your hands. In a very real sense, this prana links us together, you and me, as well as all other people and all other living things and inanimate objects. It is worth noting that the things we think of as inanimate such as tables or chairs are actually in a constant state of movement at the atomic level. The atoms that compose the wood

of the table are all in motion, but their particular rate of vibration gives the illusion of solidity. Prana is found even at this atomic level, for the atoms could not exist without it. Therefore, prana is the substratum of life, made up of countless energy units upon which the very atoms rotate and spin in their courses.

In living things, such as yourself, the prana is active and moving, whereas in dead bodies and inanimate objects, although the prana is present and does have some motion, it is either sluggish or stagnating, causing the dead body to break down and decay, and rocks or crystals to lie dormant. There is a strong link between prana and wholesome, healthy foods. Food that is as natural as possible, free from pesticides and artificial additives, is rich in vital pranic energy, but polluted foods are poor in pranic force so the pranic circulation is sluggish and somewhat stagnant. This could explain the deterioration in health among people in the West who, despite an excess of foodstuffs, often eat impure foods.

Because prana is present in oxygen molecules, it follows that when we breathe in, pranic energy circulates in the bloodstream along with the oxygen. Prana, with its mystical energy, is therefore carried to every cell in every part of the body, including those parts involved in the meditative process—the spinal cord, the brain, and the nervous system.

When we breathe using pranayama techniques, we are actually channeling the prana consciously, via the breath, and as a consequence we are bringing in more of the pranic energy than would ordinarily be the case. This is in part due to the specialized nature of the pranayama exercises and in part to the fact that the prana itself responds to thought.

Prana is a subtle energy made up of a much finer substance than the molecules that make up oxygen; prana is composed of spiritual matter (for want of a better expression). Therefore, prana, with its mystical and spiritual attributes, is finely tuned to all the thoughts and feelings that may arise from deep within you. Whatever you think of, prana flows into that thought, and whatever you feel emotionally, prana floods into that feeling. Those people who are governed by their prana may have changeable thoughts because the pranic energy behaves erratically or they may have violent or passionate tendencies because the prana is uncontrolled and has a free rein in the body. But pranayama techniques help to control and direct the

prana, turning it toward the inner, contemplative Self so that a person is released from the control of troublesome, undisciplined, and erratic thought patterns and negative emotions. By practicing pranayama you will learn to harness the prana so that, instead of rapidly moving around the body, mind, and emotions in a haphazard way, the pranic energy becomes governed, controlled, and directed.

For the vast majority of humans on this planet, the prana within their own individual systems acts like a vast flock of sheep scattered throughout the field of the body but

lacking a shepherd. A thought arises in the mind, and like sheep, the prana follows the thought and nibbles on the grass of that thought, thus reinforcing it. Suddenly you can't shake off that thought because the prana is lodged there, pasturing like sheep, over and over the same old ground. A feeling arises and, just like sheep, the prana goes into that feeling and dwells in the pasture of that emotion, so you find yourself lodged in that particular feeling. The pranic globules do not possess minds of their own; they go wherever they are drawn according to bodily functions, thought processes, and emotions. Prana carries on just like our flock of sheep, aimlessly wandering without purpose until the shepherd appears and leads the flock in another direction. You are that shepherd. Pranayama acts as both your shepherd's crook and the sheepdog. It gathers the flock together and leads it in the desired direction.

You have already mastered the technique of breath counting, so let us move on now to some more effective methods of pranic control.

PRANAYAMA PRACTICES

BREATH COUNTING WITH RETENTION OF BREATH

You are by now quite used to practicing breath counting, which has taught you how to hold the mind on one thing and to regulate the breathing in a fairly conscious way. Now I would like you to extend the exercise in breath counting by including a retention of the breath after each inhalation. What you will do now is inhale on the count of "One," then hold the inspired air in the lungs. Experiment with a time duration (lasting only seconds) that feels comfortable to you. For the average person I would suggest that four or five seconds of retention is adequate at first. The next step is to release the breath gently in a slow and controlled manner, and then begin the cycle again with "Two," the next inhalation, and repeat the process until the fourth breath, then start again at "One."

Remember that the inhalations and exhalations are all done through the nostrils, not the open mouth. The benefits of pranayama are greatly enhanced when done via the nostrils. There are many reasons for this. The air is warmed and humidified as it passes through the nasal conchae and turbinates (the bony portions of the nasal cavity), and the airflow over these nasal bones creates turbulence that precipitates dust and other airborne particles against the nasal surfaces, where they become stuck in the mucus that covers the nasal turbinates. These foreign particles are removed by filamentlike cells known as cilia, which line the nasal walls and pulsate in waves, gradually moving the mucus and entrapped particles toward the throat to be swallowed and disposed of in the gut. These are the healthy reasons to breathe nasally. But there is another reason for nasal breathing. The pranic molecules can come into direct contact with the nerves in the upper palate and thus travel directly to the brain via these nerves, particularly the vagus or tenth cranial nerve.

THE VAGUS (TENTH CRANIAL) NERVE

What is so important about the vagus nerve? Well, the vagus is part of the parasympathetic nervous system, the system of the major nerves known as cranial nerves because they branch out from the brain stem. Without going into too much unnecessary detail for the purposes of a book of this nature, I will outline only those aspects that interest us as meditators. I suggest referring to a good-quality anatomy and physiology book if you want more detailed information.

The vagus nerve is the chief nerve of the parasympathetic nervous system, and about 70 percent of the nerve fibers of this system have their origins in the vagus. The vagus supplies nerve fibers to the lungs, heart, and virtually all of the abdominal organs, and although the other cranial nerves supply other regions of the body, we must bear in mind that the vagus is the main governing nerve over all of the others. Therefore, the vagus represents the parasympathetic nervous system itself. The vagus, either directly via its own nerve fibers or indirectly via the other cranial nerves, has effects on the pupil of the eye, the secretion of digestive juices, the sweat glands, and the heart and other organs.

Parasympathetic stimuli from the vagus decrease the activity of the heart, which is very interesting in relation to meditational practice, for during meditation the heart rate slows down greatly. In fact, some Indian gurus have managed to slow the heart so much that it seems to all appearances they have died. However, you need not worry about any danger, because it takes extreme practices to slow the heart down to a virtual cessation of its beat, and the techniques in this book will not lead you into any such peril. But the heart rate will slow, or rather calm down, as a result of pranayama techniques, which is very beneficial, physically, emotionally, and mentally. Top athletes often have a slower heart rate than that of other people, and they are unusually fit specimens who suffer no ill-effects from a reduced heart rate and slower pulse, and in fact enjoy better health.

Think about how you feel when you are short of breath. Everyday circumstances can cause irregular breathing and increased heart rate, but so can negative thoughts and emotions. To demonstrate how our thoughts and feelings affect physiological processes, cast your mind back to your most embarrassing moment, if you have ever had one. Think about it. What happened? Did you perhaps feel your face flushing red? If you did, that is an example of how thought can affect you bodily.

If that didn't work for you, or if you don't have anything particularly embarrassing locked away in your past, then try another exercise. Check your pulse and count how many pulses there are to a minute by looking at a clock or watch. Now, think of something that has made you angry. Then after a little while, check your pulse again. I'll bet it's faster than it was previously.

These experiments demonstrate how thoughts and feelings can affect our entire being, even the body itself. Our pranayama exercises will combat these harmful effects and help us eliminate many of the negative attitudes that we still hold on to from the past.

DIGITAL PRANAYAMA

In this method of pranayama we use the fingers of one hand (usually the right hand, although the left is fine) to control the flow of breath through the nostrils. You will be pleasantly surprised how uplifting this practice can be if you follow the technique correctly. I advise that you listen to the recorded exercise on the Meditation CD, and follow my voice, for the first few sessions. The exercise is timed to last 5 minutes—the recommended duration to begin with.

Seat yourself in a comfortable position, preferably on the floor on a cushion (ideally in the Lotus or Half Lotus position—see page 18) or, if you prefer, on a chair that has no armrests that could interfere with the practice. Rest the left hand on the left knee if you are seated crossed-legged or in the Lotus or Half Lotus. If you are in a chair, rest the left hand on the upper left thigh.

Before you begin, it is a good idea to blow your nose and clear out any nasal obstructions so that the airways are clear.

The index, middle, and ring fingers are folded into the palm.

Begin your practice by taking a few regular breaths to relax yourself and create the right frame of mind. Expel the breath through both of your nostrils.

Raise the right hand and bring it up to your face, leaving a gap between the armpit and the body so that the arm feels comfortable. Now fold the index, middle, and ring fingers into the palm of the hand. With your fingers thus positioned, close off the right nostril with the thumb, (if using your left hand you will be closing off with the little finger) and breathe in only via the left nostril for a count of four seconds.

When using the right hand, the left nostril is closed with the little finger.

Close the left nostril with the little finger (and ring finger, if you prefer), keeping the thumb

The thumb of the right hand is used to close the right nostril.

With the left nostril closed, expel the breath through the right nostril.

closed over the right nostril. Hold the breath for a count of eight seconds. Release the pressure of the thumb and let the air expel from the right nostril for a count of six seconds.

Reverse the whole process, by breathing in again, only this time via the right nostril for a count of four seconds. Close the thumb over the right nostril and once more hold the breath for a count of eight seconds. Release the pressure of the little finger from the left nostril and let the air out for a count of six seconds.

This practice equals one round of digital pranayama. To recap, we have the flow of breath through the left nostril, holding it, and expelling it through the right nostril. We breathe in again through the right nostril, hold the breath again, and expel it through the left nostril. This completes one round. We shall aim for five rounds initially.

Even if you are worried that breathing in this manner will be far too difficult or that breath holding is impossible for eight seconds, I ask you to persevere, for the results are worthwhile.

A good method for keeping track of the rounds is to count on the left hand while the right hand is doing the digital pranayama. Use the fingers of the left hand as markers, beginning with the index finger on the first joint on the thumb counting as Round 1, then the same finger on the tip of the thumb as Round 2, then the tip of the middle finger on the tip of the thumb as Round 3, then the tip of the ring finger on the tip of the thumb as Round 4, and finally the tip of the little finger on the thumb as Round 5. This method sets your mind free to concentrate solely on counting the length of the breaths without worrying about the rounds.

In time, you will be able to increase the numbers of rounds to ten and beyond, and also increase the length of time spent on each breath sequence. Perhaps after several weeks or months have passed, you will breathe in to a count of eight, hold for a count of 16 seconds, and breathe out for a count of 8 seconds. Beyond this, you will probably find your own comfortable level and dispense with counting the breaths altogether. I never count my own breaths now, and haven't done so for many years. With continued practice, you will sense the limit of your own capacity. What is good and feels right for one person may not feel right for another, so experiment.

However, I would ask you never to exceed a comfortable level in any drastic way. Pushing ahead too quickly and trying to force yourself will not have desirable effects, and instead of emerging from digital pranayama feeling uplifted, you will feel agitated. Patience and comfortable practice are required, not charging in forcefully. Discover your own digital pranayama breath-counting routine. You may find that a count of 2, 6, 4, is better than the given 4, 8, 6, or that when you are more experienced, holding the breath for a count of 16 is asking too much of your lung capacity, so trim that to perhaps a count of 8, 12, 8. Maybe the out-breath count is too long and you find it exasperating. Trim it down, and decide what works for you. If the in-breath count feels too long or not long enough, reduce or extend the breath accordingly. There should be no rigid rules. The main point of the exercise is to focus comfortably.

You will eventually forget about counting the breathing sequences and will naturally breathe according to your own capacity, concentrating on the flow of the excercise.

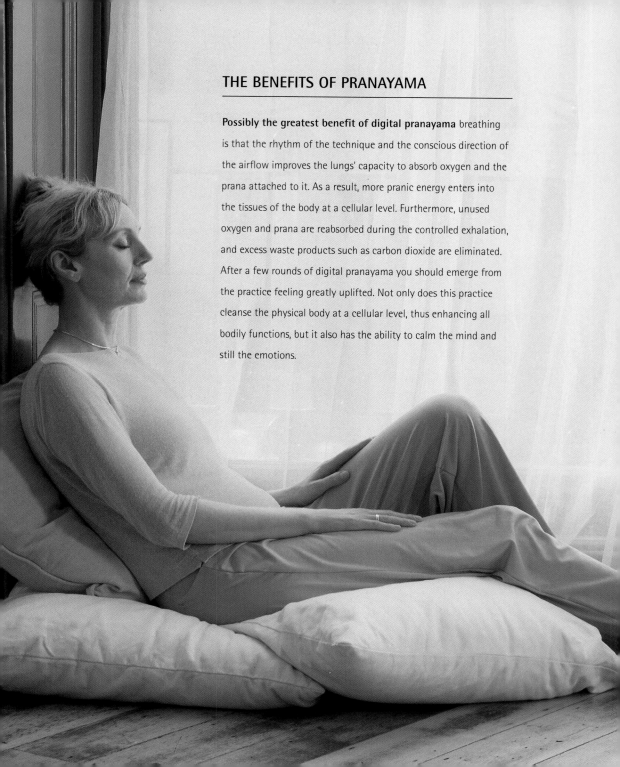

THE BENEFITS OF PRANAYAMA

Possibly the greatest benefit of digital pranayama breathing
is that the rhythm of the technique and the conscious direction of
the airflow improves the lungs' capacity to absorb oxygen and the
prana attached to it. As a result, more pranic energy enters into
the tissues of the body at a cellular level. Furthermore, unused
oxygen and prana are reabsorbed during the controlled exhalation,
and excess waste products such as carbon dioxide are eliminated.
After a few rounds of digital pranayama you should emerge from
the practice feeling greatly uplifted. Not only does this practice
cleanse the physical body at a cellular level, thus enhancing all
bodily functions, but it also has the ability to calm the mind and
still the emotions.

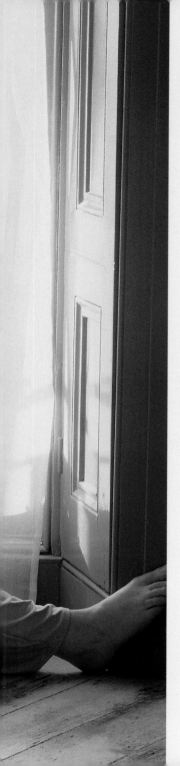

It does this by relaxing the nervous system and cleansing it of toxins. I have a theory, which is yet to be scientifically proven, that pranayama breathing techniques such as this may even play a role in eliminating disease-producing free radicals from the body. Free radicals, which are present in every person's body, are atoms that contain unpaired electrons. These atoms are unstable and must steal electrons from stable atoms. Oxygen plays a role in the stability or instability of atoms, and I therefore believe that pranayama breathing may assist in the elimination of free radicals.

But, theories aside, pranayama will positively help to cleanse and heal the body, still the mind, and steady the emotions. You will most definitely feel that you have greater clarity of thought and yet a calmer, less ruffled mind. Negative emotions such as anger, fear, and sorrow will dissolve, or at least quiet down, giving you the ability to handle them, and feelings such as despair or depression will seem to lift away from you. Mentally, you will discover a greater ability for focused attention on one thing, and your powers of concentration will seem vastly enhanced. Your relationships with others will improve, because you will be more willing to meet them halfway, and if other individuals still prove unwilling to cooperate with you, or are behaving unreasonably, at least your own attitude toward them will have significantly and positively improved.

Obviously, all of these wonderful results will not happen after a single session of digital pranayama. You must keep up a daily practice. However, even after the first attempt, I can guarantee that your head will feel clearer and your emotions calmer. Continuous practice will help your meditation and will assist you in achieving your goals, whatever they may be.

5: the sacred aum

The techniques outlined in this chapter are intended to lead you into the actual process of entering the truly meditative state. Up until now, we have been dealing with concentration practices for achieving a point of mental focus, and with exercises that induce a feeling of calm, well-being, and mind stilling. We have reached the section of the book dealing with meditation itself, which enables us to achieve a state transcending everyday consciousness. We are now seeking not simply to have a focused mind, calm thoughts or pleasant feelings, but to rise above the everyday thought processes.

The term "meditation" is not easily definable, for meditation involves many levels or layers that are reached progressively as one descends deeper into the Self. Each of us is unique, and each individual will learn meditation in his or her own way and at his or her own pace. Yet clearly, we must mark a point wherein meditation begins

even if it is at a very tentative stage of our practice. The problem with definition arises because concentration often merges with the state of meditation itself, for the one state leads progressively into the other. Basically, concentration leads to meditation. It might be best understood that meditation begins when the thoughts of everyday have become subdued and have fallen below the threshold of consciousness, bringing with it a stillness to the mind that is not commonly experienced in normal day-to-day circumstances. This chapter is intended to lead you somewhat toward that state, and from now on we should consider that we are practicing meditational techniques.

MANTRAS

Mantras are specialized sounds that an individual gives voice to in order to attain certain states of consciousness. There are many hundreds of mantras, most of which originate from the ancient Sanskrit texts of India and are supposed to invoke the aid of Indian deities. Ultimately, all mantras are said to be invocations of the Supreme Being or God. Whatever your beliefs, the important thing is to be sincere and focused when using a mantra.

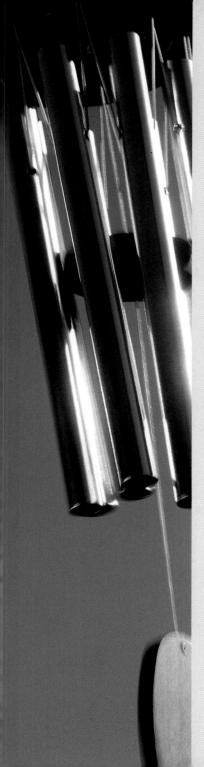

Many people claim that the particular mantra they use is the best and most effective, and most of them disagree with one another. There are so many gurus and mantras that it is easy to become confused. I would not disregard anyone else's claims, but at the same time I would not accept those claims blindly. Personally, I have found that many of the mantras are so long and complicated that they are a hindrance to a focused and still mind and are often very difficult to pronounce correctly, especially for Western people.

In my own personal experience, I have discovered that it is far better to use just one universal mantra that is simple, uncomplicated, and has a regular rhythm that can be focused upon exclusively. There is no other mantra that fulfills all of these requirements quite as well as the OM, or AUM, mantra.

AUM is said to be the highest mantra of all, and I believe rightly so. No other mantra affects the psyche, or indeed, the entire being like the AUM does. AUM has purificatory effects upon the physical body, the emotions, and the mind. Sounding this powerful mantra takes the process of pranayama a step farther, leading you beyond into the realms of the inner Self, the soul, where meditation should ultimately lead us all. When repeated as part of your meditation technique, AUM will gradually eradicate lower, selfish desires and wants, cleansing and purifying the thoughts, thus improving the actual quality of your thoughts, as well as helping to eliminate negative emotional traits.

AUM is able to destroy unwanted thoughts by breaking down the thought patterns that produced them in the first place, whether those negative thought patterns arose from the emotions or from the mind itself. In this way, AUM acts like ultrasound, in that it has the capacity, via its resonance, to break down the basic components of thoughts and emotions that are not conducive to wholeness.

I realize that these are weighty claims, but AUM must be experienced to be understood. I am not saying that on your first few attempts at sounding the AUM mantra all your troubles and cares will be broken down and eliminated and that you will find yourself projected into a higher state of consciousness! Yet with time, patience, determination, and practice, you will see a gradual change in many aspects of your persona (physical, emotional, and mental) and will over time recognize positive developments in all or most areas of your being.

AUM is the very note of God, and whether you believe in a Supreme Being or not, or don't know either way, it hardly matters, for AUM contains its own inherent wisdom and truth, regardless of what the finite mind believes or does not believe. AUM is universal, and like the sun, sheds its light upon all without judgment. But that is the spiritual side of things. Let's now consider the mechanics of producing this mystical and practical sound.

THE AUM TECHNIQUE

On first attempting the AUM technique, you may struggle. Ignore any difficulties, and press on regardless. Keep practicing and before long you will be producing a wonderfully resonant sound.

Seat yourself comfortably, as you would for breath counting, or pranayama. Close your eyes and breathe regularly through the nose until you feel relaxed and at ease. If you choose, accompany my voice on the CD until you feel comfortable on your own. Start by just humming with a fairly strong, clearly audible sound. Let the hum be tuneless and feel it vibrating into the top of your head. Don't worry if you don't feel any vibration at this stage. Take a breath and hum again until the breath is exhausted (without straining of course) and begin again, making a regular, steady hum that feels as if it is rising into the skull itself. Continue in this steady way. Remember that the hum has no tune. It is a steady hum, like that of an electrical appliance such as a refrigerator, tuneless and repetitive.

After a few minutes, and only if you feel ready, see if you can extend this sound by drawing it up from the navel under the diaphragm at the base of the lower ribs, in a deeper, more resonant tone. Take an in-breath first, and use the air intake to produce the sound. After the in-breath, begin to sound the AUM with open mouth, beginning right down from the very pit of the navel, trying to feel the sound. Draw the sound upward, directing it into the throat and over the larynx and upward to the upper palate. From here the AUM vibrates from the roof of the mouth into the head. Finally, the sound ends with the lips closing in a soft hum. Try it again: breathe in deeply through the nose, open the mouth, and begin the sound with the "AU" of AUM. Let the "AU" (sounds like the "au" of audition) be prolonged so that the sound carries right up from the navel and through the chest area into the throat and upward to resonate upon the sounding board of the upper palate.

As the lips begin to close, sound the hum of the "M" and allow this sound to extend in an elongated hum until the breath has been expended. Then try again. Try about ten AUMs at first, or fewer if that is too much, and then notice how you feel.

At first you may not notice much of an effect, which could perhaps be the result of incorrect practice. Pronounced correctly, AUM has noticeable effects. But don't be discouraged if you don't experience much initially, just practice and stay with it. Remember that discipline is essential in all meditation techniques, and staying with the practice is what brings the benefit. Most people enjoy the AUM, and if you don't when you begin to practice, you probably will as your proficiency increases.

AUM is one of the best tonics for strengthening the nervous system, and even when pronounced mentally without making any sound, it has power. Sounding the AUM will sharpen your concentration and improve the quality and content of your meditation.

Having been given all this information about the AUM, you may be thinking to yourself, "Yes. But how exactly can a sound like AUM have such profound effects upon me? After all, it is only a sound, isn't it?" AUM is much more than just a sound. It is an energy, and it affects a very special gland nestled in the brain, called the pituitary.

THE PITUITARY GLAND AND THE AUM

The pituitary gland sits at the base of the brain in a position that is aligned with the space between the eyes. According to some, the pituitary is the physical seat of the soul, which is an interesting symbolism since the eyes are said to be the mirror of the soul. In a sense then, the eyes reflect the pituitary gland and reveal its level of development. It is a curious thing that spiritually inclined people often have remarkable eyes that are large, open, clear, and beautiful. This is a direct result of their high level of spiritual evolution; when the pituitary gland is finely balanced and functioning effectively (particularly at levels beyond the purely physical), its healthy state shines through the eyes.

This special gland is found in a bony cavity of the skull known as the *sella turcica*, which is Latin for "Turk's saddle," because the cavity literally resembles a Turkish riding saddle. This is another curious symbolism, because stimulation of the pituitary by sounding the AUM and other meditational techniques causes the inner Self or soul to "ride" into higher consciousness.

The *sella turcica* is part of a larger bony portion of the floor of the skull called the sphenoid bone. The sphenoid bone is shaped like two wings and the *sella turcica* sits between these two wings with the pituitary resting within. So, the pituitary not only "rides" upon the *sella turcica*, it also "flies" upon the sphenoid. In higher states of consciousness induced by the techniques of meditation, the soul takes flight.

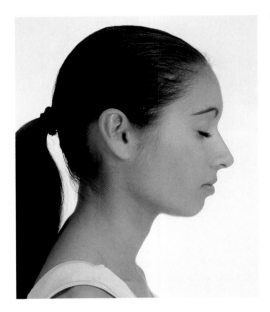

The natural structures of the body seem to reflect these inherent truths about the nature of our spiritual reality. Deep secrets are hidden or disguised within the natural world, waiting for us to discover them. It's as if the Supreme Being is playing a game of hide and seek with us. The truth we seek so desperately is there, but it is cleverly hidden from view, like those trick illustrations that contain hidden pictures of animals camouflaged within the scenery. The game is to find these truths. The location of the pituitary is a prime example of such a discovery.

The pituitary and its bony socket are found immediately beneath the hypothalamus of the brain. The hypothalamus controls hunger and thirst and regulates body temperature. The pituitary gland itself is composed of two parts: the anterior pituitary and the posterior pituitary. Because the pituitary is an endocrine gland, that is, a gland that secretes hormones into the bloodstream, it plays a vital part in how the body functions and how the individual relates to his or her body.

The pituitary is the master over all the other endocrine glands and releases hormones that govern the rate of growth of all cells in the body; it regulates the thyroid gland found at the base of the throat, the rate of secretions of the adrenal glands, and controls the level of sex hormones. The physiological functions of the pituitary gland are immense and far-reaching, so I will try to keep my descriptions brief. If you wish to discover more about how our glands affect the body and the emotions, I suggest you refer to a good anatomy and physiology book.

The pituitary gland is connected to the brain itself, unlike the other endocrine glands that it governs. It is really an extension of the hypothalamus and is attached to the former by the hypophyseal stalk. It is perhaps worth noting with reference to our observations of the connection between the eyes and the pituitary gland that the optic chiasma is found in the hypothalamus and has close links with the pituitary via blood supply and nerve plexuses. This is another factor that seems to support my belief that the state of the pituitary gland is reflected through the eyes.

So, how does all this anatomical information relate to our practice of meditation? Well, it's like this: when one is utilizing the AUM in meditational practice, the intoned AUM reverberating in the skull causes the sphenoid bone to vibrate, which in turn sets up a vibration in the *sella turcica*; this in turn gently vibrates the pituitary gland. This gentle stimulus assists greatly in regulating the functioning of this special gland. When you consider the far-reaching consequences of the healthy stimulus of the pituitary, it makes practical sense to use the AUM mantra regularly (either with my voice on the CD or on your own) as a part of a natural health regime.

THE PINEAL GLAND

The pituitary gland is not the only endocrine gland in the cavity of the skull. There is another, lesser-known gland, called the pineal, which sits between the two hemispheres of the brain, more or less in the middle of it, just above and behind the pituitary gland.

Although little is known scientifically about the pineal, I would suggest that, in time and with more research, this endocrine gland will prove to be the master over all the glands, including the pituitary gland. If the pituitary gland corresponds to the soul, then the pineal must correspond to the over soul, or the higher Self, a still greater aspect of the individual reality. I believe that in the vast majority of human beings the pineal is in a more or less atrophied state and does not perform at its full potential. But I also believe that in an individual who has gained a certain measure of spiritual development (and I do not mean just being kind and decent) the pineal gland awakens and reveals itself, resulting in a higher state of consciousness. Such an individual has what may be called "soul qualities."

It seems that the sound of AUM not only stimulates the pituitary but also has a natural side effect of awakening the pineal from its dormant sleep. The sound of AUM reverberates on the pituitary gland, and the gentle stimulus in turn knocks

softly at the door of the pineal gland, slowly and gradually awakening it into activity. Such an awakening opens the way for the pineal to demonstrate its faculties, which at the moment are largely mysterious and hidden from science. I believe that this gentle and safe awakening helps a person to contact the higher Self or to attain God consciousness or enlightenment as it is often called in the East. This awakening does not happen overnight and is not drastic or dangerous. Its progress is slow, almost imperceptible, yet as surely as water dripping upon a stone will one day wear away that stone, so the awakening of the pineal gland will eventually wear away the barriers to enlightenment.

In AUM technique you have a tool that acts like the pick that our caver might use to scale the difficult rocks. As you explore the inner world, the AUM tool can assist in your ascent over all obstacles along the way and help you chip away at untried ledges to gain a foothold toward higher ground. Use the AUM every time you meditate or when you are distressed, unhappy, or angry, or simply in need of energy. If particular circumstances make the sounding of the AUM unfeasible, remember that you can use AUM *mentally*. As you do so, try to feel the energy of AUM entering the skull just as if you were sounding the AUM mantra verbally. Whether you use the AUM audibly or mentally, it will quickly uplift your spirits and bring you fresh inspiration and a feeling of release and freedom.

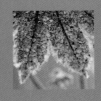

6: the chakras

Chances are that a person who is interested in meditation will already have some knowledge about the chakras, but for those readers who are unfamiliar with the concept, I will provide a brief summary.

Discussion about the chakras or "energy centers" move us into deeply esoteric territory, but I do not feel that meditational knowledge or experience would be complete without a basic understanding of the concept of the chakras and energy fields. Nevertheless, it is up to you to decide whether the following discourse is true, false, or somewhere in the middle.

ENERGY FIELDS

I think that most of my readers would agree that humans are not just a physical conglomeration of cells that constitute a tangible body. We are more than that, as indeed are all living things. It is generally accepted among those interested in spiritual matters that a person has several bodies that coexist in subtle form or substance and each one interpenetrates and radiates out from the physical body. These subtle bodies form an energy field around the physical body.

Images of these energy fields or "auras" can be captured on film using a specialized photographic process known as Kirlian photography. There exist tens of thousands of such photographs, and you may well have seen some of them yourself. I have a Kirlian photograph of my own hand, showing the energy lines emanating from it. There are Kirlian photographs showing auras around leaves, flowers, pieces of bread, and even coins. Everything—both living and inanimate—has an energy field emanating from it.

The energy field around the physical body is made up of several subtle bodies: the etheric body (the one Kirlian photography is able to capture on film), the emotional or astral body, the mental body, and beyond that the higher, spiritual bodies. There is a great deal of debate over the subtle bodies, which are often labeled differently by various schools of thought. For our purposes, suffice it to say that we have several subtle bodies that we use to express ourselves. (To go beyond this would require another book because the subject is so complex and vast.) Since each of us operates within these bodies, including the physical one, whatever originates in one body will affect all of the others to varying degrees. This interaction between the bodies occurs via the chakras.

THE SEVEN CHAKRAS

The word chakra is the Sanskrit word for a "wheel." Chakras are revolving with energy, for each one is a vortex of force. These vortexes direct various types of energy spiraling up or down the various bodies and between them.

There are seven main chakras located in the subtle bodies, and each one of them corresponds to areas of the physical spinal cord and nerve plexuses. Each chakra also corresponds to the endocrine system.

1 The lowest chakra, called *Muladhara* in Sanskrit, is found at the base of the spinal column and is associated with the sacral plexus. It is known as the Base Chakra.
2 Next, ascending up the spinal cord, we have the *Swadhistana* chakra, which corresponds to the prostatic plexus. This chakra is associated with the gonads in the male and the ovaries in the female. This vortex is the Sacral Chakra.
3 At the region of the navel we find the *Manipura* chakra. It is linked to the solar plexus and the adrenal glands and pancreas. It is also called the Solar Plexus Chakra.
4 At the heart there is the *Anahata* chakra. It is associated with the cardiac plexus and the thymus gland. It is the Heart Chakra.

The seven chakras are invisible vortexes of energy that act as points of interaction between the physical and subtle bodies.

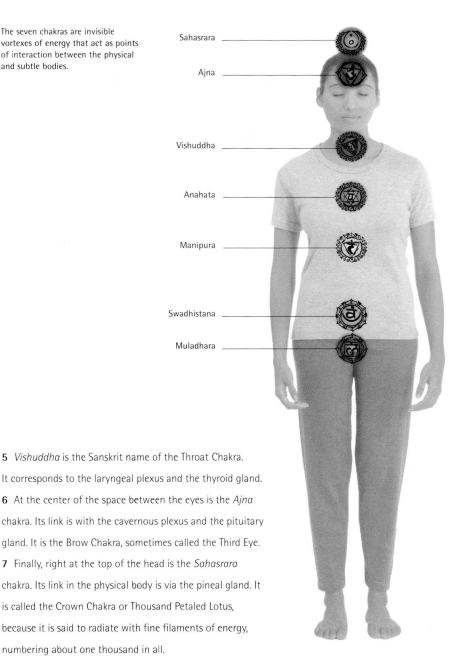

Sahasrara

Ajna

Vishuddha

Anahata

Manipura

Swadhistana

Muladhara

5 *Vishuddha* is the Sanskrit name of the Throat Chakra. It corresponds to the laryngeal plexus and the thyroid gland.

6 At the center of the space between the eyes is the *Ajna* chakra. Its link is with the cavernous plexus and the pituitary gland. It is the Brow Chakra, sometimes called the Third Eye.

7 Finally, right at the top of the head is the *Sahasrara* chakra. Its link in the physical body is via the pineal gland. It is called the Crown Chakra or Thousand Petaled Lotus, because it is said to radiate with fine filaments of energy, numbering about one thousand in all.

All of the chakras are said to resemble lotus flowers, according to the Eastern schools of thought, and are therefore often referred to as lotuses. There are many more minor chakras throughout the etheric body, such as one in the palm of each hand and one at the back of the head. Our focus of attention is upon the seven major chakras.

Each of these seven chakras, or "energy centers" as they are often called in the West, is said to correspond in ascending order to the color spectrum or rainbow. Starting with the lower frequency of the spectrum, the Base Chakra is seen as a red vibrational energy, and moving up the spinal cord, the Sacral Chakra is orange, the Solar Plexus Chakra is yellow, the Heart Chakra is green, the Throat Chakra is blue, the Brow Chakra is indigo, and the Crown Chakra is purple.

These color associations are a generalization based upon the normal state of the average person. However, chakra colors can change according to mood and temperament and especially spiritual evolution. If someone is angry, upset, or in pain, the colors can become dull and lackluster. If the person is happy the energy centers vibrate more fully, and the chakra colors shine out sharper and brighter.

THE CROWN CHAKRA

Those who are gifted with seeing the aura and the chakras claim that a spiritually evolved individual has brilliant white or golden light in the energy centers, particularly at the Crown Chakra. Artists throughout the ages and in many cultures have depicted saints and sages with golden halos around the head. They may not have actually seen these halos for themselves, but they were probably following a long tradition established by those who had seen such golden auras.

When a person has generated enough love energy and acquired a certain degree of wisdom and understanding of spiritual realities, then the Crown Chakra seems to "open up" like a lotus flower unfolding. This opening of the Crown Chakra gradually changes the radiance in that center, and the tiny, fine filaments of the Thousand Petal Lotus turn from their normal purple into brilliant white and gold hues. During meditation and at other uplifting times, there is often a sense that this chakra is opening. Listening to beautiful, devotional type music may have an opening effect upon the Crown Chakra. I have often felt my own crown center opening and glowing and can honestly say that in those moments I feel transformed. As experience increases, this sensation becomes more apparent and more frequent. It brings spiritual inspiration and a sense of great love and wisdom. It must be experienced to be truly comprehended. I can only say that this experience surpasses anything ordinary everyday life has to offer.

Everyone is capable of opening up the Crown Chakra, and, by degrees, it opens up in all spiritually minded people according to their particular stage of spiritual evolution. When the Crown Chakra fully opens in a truly enlightened being, the whole of the personality is transcended and the inner light or radiant Self is witnessed and fully expressed. The best example that I can think of regarding this transcendental experience is the transfiguration of Jesus Christ. We read in the Gospel of Luke, 9:29, that Jesus and his disciples Peter, John, and James all went up into a mountain to pray, "and as Jesus prayed, the fashion of his countenance was altered, and his raiment was white and glistening." The same account is given in Matthew 17:2, "and [he] was transfigured before them: and his face did shine as the sun, and his raiment was white as the light." According to the Gospel of Mark, 9:2–3, "He was transfigured before them. And his raiment became shining, exceeding white as snow; whiter than anyone on earth can bleach them."

exceeding white as snow; whiter than anyone on earth can bleach them."

All these biblical accounts tell us that Jesus of Nazareth was radiating the inner light of the soul that is found within the higher spiritual bodies, and through this spiritual energy he purified even his material physical body. His face "did shine as the sun" because the Crown Chakra energy was flooding from his head. Even his clothing seemed to shine with this radiant light, such is the power of this transformation.

I am not suggesting that this incredible experience will happen to you, so don't be alarmed. On the other hand, don't be disappointed if it doesn't! What these accounts do suggest (from a nonreligious viewpoint) is that the chakras are real and the energy we work with in our meditations is real and can actually be sensed vibrationally. Without a doubt, as the Crown Chakra opens, you will have some very blissful and deep experiences that will, in their own gradual and safe way, transfigure your lower nature into a higher and better state of being. You will be changing consciousness.

THE NADIS

In addition to the chakras or energy centers, there are tubelike connections in etheric matter that link the chakras to one another and through which energy flows in the form of prana. These etheric tubes are called *nadis* in Sanskrit; or in the singular each tube is known as a nadi. The nadis carry psychic currents throughout the etheric body; they act a bit like blood vessels carrying blood or lymph vessels transporting lymphatic substance throughout the body. Traditional Indian paintings

We need not go into detail about the nadis, but there are three important nadis worth mentioning; these are known in Sanskrit as the *Ida*, *Pingala*, and *Sushumna* nadis, and they interconnect all the seven main chakras.

The most important of these is the Sushumna nadi, which runs up the central canal of the spinal cord. It is said that at the final liberation or emancipation, the fully illuminated soul receives a rush of spiritual energy (*kundalini* in Sanskrit) that flows up from Muladhara, the Base Chakra, purifies all of the other chakras, and then radiates out of the Crown Chakra. The Sushumna nadi carries this kundalini energy. Kundalini is said to be the primordial cosmic energy of the universe, the basic creative force that shapes all things anew, transforming them. It was probably the kundalini that transformed Christ and flooded out of his Crown Chakra.

In the average person the kundalini energy is said to lie dormant, coiled up like a serpent at Muladhara, the Base Chakra, and is awakened only through spiritual training and disciplines. It is my belief that kundalini does not necessarily burst up through all seven chakras in a blinding flash of light. That may be the case for some individuals, but I think it is more usual for this spiritual energy to transform the individual gradually over a long period of time. I am not one who holds that spiritual enlightenment must come in the metaphorical "blinding flash of light" as it did for St. Paul on the road to Damascus.

BLINDING LIGHT

It is worth considering that too much light all at once can indeed be "blinding." That is the operative word. A blinding light produces the sudden fanatic who is blinded to all other truths and all other ideas. You need only read the Letters of St. Paul in the New Testament to grasp my meaning. Bear in mind, also, that Paul had been fanatically opposed to Christianity and devoted to Judaism prior to his Road to Damascus experience. His single-mindedness and narrow beliefs were merely transferred to a different creed. This observation may upset some people of the Christian faith, but I make no apologies. Only the *gradual* emerging of light truly illumines and reveals the truth. Can you see clearly if you have been in the pitch black and suddenly have a brilliant light shone in your eyes? Clear sight is developed only when the intensity of the light comes in slowly and gradually, allowing the eyes to adjust. It is the same for spiritual realities: truth and wisdom that are developed over

time with patience and persistence will ultimately be better understood and more deeply held. The slow-growing oak tree stands the test of time: although the quickly sprouting spring flowers may be pretty, they are gone in a few days. What we are hoping to build in meditation is something that will stand the test of time and all of life's vicissitudes, so that each spiritual practice can build upon the last. We should see ourselves as strong oak trees that can endure the insults and troubles of life, rather than pretty flowers that are here today and gone tomorrow, wilting at the first frost.

Meditation is meant to build your character, and the consistent efforts that you put in will reap rewards in the long run. The goal is not to experience a "blinding light" but to stay with your discipline regardless of the frustrations. The art of sitting for meditation is the goal, and that is difficult enough for most people. Yet this very discipline of regular practice will bring its own rewards. Do not expect a Road to Damascus experience; it probably won't happen. If it does, fine. Accept it with good grace. However, be sure that the light is not blinding. You will have your experiences in meditation, and many of them will no doubt be blissful, beautiful, and uplifting.

You will gain inner knowledge that comes from the realms of the soul. All this and more may come to you in time. But most of the time your meditations will feel routine, sometimes even boring or uneventful. You must then summon up all of your discipline to stay with it, because no session of meditation is wasted. You are like the oak tree that grows strong by slowly and consistently growing layer upon layer. Although the rate of growth may be imperceptible, it leads to strength and stability. In the same way, consistent meditation leads to spiritual growth and stability.

On either side of the Sushumna lie the Ida and Pingala nadis: the Ida is on the left side, and the Pingala is on the right. The Ida nadi directs energy through the left nostril, and the Pingala nadi directs energy, or prana, through the right nostril. During digital pranayama practice, the pranic current generated by the breath purifies the nadis. This purification process eliminates psychic debris that has accumulated over time in these nadis. Psychic debris is the stagnated waste from negative emotions such as fear, hatred, envy, grief, and all other kinds of negative states. Channeled breathing through the nostrils carries prana along with it and cleanses the Ida and Pingala, and holding the breath cleanses the Sushumna.

Digital pranayama in particular will enable you to raise the kundalini energy safely and gradually in a natural and intelligent way. You may have heard alarming stories of the kundalini being aroused and causing damage to the individual, either physically, emotionally, or mentally. As far as I know, there are no documented cases of this occurring, and if it has happened, it must have been the result of some very peculiar and dangerous practices indeed. The methods of pranayama breathing that I have shown you, and the sensible, sane approach to meditation that you are learning from this book, will not harm you at all but will only enhance your quality of life. Kundalini arises naturally as the individual progresses spiritually, and these techniques are safe tools to aid in that process. It's like a trainee sprinter who chooses the correct running shoes; the shoes help, but it is the person who must actually do the running. The spiritual quest is the same: these techniques will not bring about spirituality or altered states of consciousness—that comes only when the inner Self reveals itself—but the pranayama breathing will assist in the purification and focusing process, like good running shoes keeping you on track.

ENERGIZING THE CHAKRAS

The chakras can be energized by vocalizing the AUM mantra. Begin with a few rounds of digital pranayama, perhaps followed by five minutes of candle gazing. Now close your eyes and see if you can visualize a bright golden light, like a candle flame, at the base of the spine at the Base Chakra. Breathe steadily in through the nostrils and out through the nostrils in a regular and relaxed rhythm. The breaths should be long, deep, and fairly slow. Visualize the Base Chakra beginning to glow and grow in size until it seems to shine like a bright and brilliant sun. After a few moments, or whenever you feel ready, sound the AUM with concentration upon the Base Chakra. Feel the energy that is generated rising up the spine and entering into the Sacral Chakra. Use exactly the same techniques as for the Base Chakra and sound the AUM in the Sacral Chakra when ready.

Repeat this process as you move upward into the Solar Plexus Chakra, and continue on up the spine to the Heart Chakra, the Throat Chakra, the Brow Chakra, and finally the Crown Chakra. At the Crown, you may wish to linger a little longer, visualizing the brilliance of the light radiating out from the head as far as you can. Try sounding the AUM at least three times or more at the Crown Chakra.

This is a very powerful meditation technique, and when you are more experienced it can even be extended to last for a full half hour or so if you feel like it, taking up the whole of an average meditation session. For example, you may wish to begin by sitting for meditation, and instead of candle gazing or breath counting, you might try dispensing with those practices and replacing them with a few rounds of digital pranayama, and then go directly into chakra visualization and resonating the AUM in each of the chakras. Once you have been meditating regularly, your intuition will guide you toward using those techniques that will help you most at any one time. AUM sounded in the chakras has a cleansing and balancing effect, and can be quite a blissful experience. Don't worry if it isn't though. Just keep practicing.

The mind is the most powerful tool we have, and the body and emotions are directly affected by our constant thoughts. If you continually tell yourself that you are unhappy, it will not be long before you actually feel quite awful inwardly, moving from mild upset to deep melancholia. Then even the physical body becomes ill, susceptible to viruses, etc. If on the other hand, you tell yourself you are happy, then before long you will actually begin to feel happy inside. The physical body of a truly happy person seems to be vibrant and glowing.

In the same way, when we visualize light as an energy flowing within us, we draw more of the inner, spiritual light into our psyche, and after some time, perhaps even just a little time, we start to feel that we are changing, purifying at many levels, and becoming more balanced and at one within.

BEING AT ONE

Think about that expression of being "at one." If you join the two words together you have "atone." According to one dictionary, atone means "to make amends or reparation" and "to be in or bring into agreement." That is what we are trying to do in meditation. We are attempting to "make amends" for all that has gone before that we do not like about ourselves, whatever that may be. We are also trying to "be in agreement" with the higher Self, which is the true Self. We are in the process of becoming AT ONE. We are preparing to ATONE for all that has been negative about ourselves and thus to emerge as fuller, more enlightened beings.

7: the stillness within

Let us recap what we have learned so far. Following our caver analogy, we have begun to use various tools on our journey into the depths of the cave of the inner Self, and in using these tools we are becoming experienced in the mystical realms of meditation. We have learned to count our breaths, candle gaze, and perform digital pranayama, including suspending the breath with conscious control, and we have discovered how the breath and the mind are interrelated. In addition, we have begun to realize how meditative techniques affect the physical body as well as the mind and emotions. We have learned to use the mystical AUM to energize the chakras. We now understand that we have several subtle bodies and that the chakras are force centers that emanate from those finer bodies.

If you are a complete beginner to meditation, then this has been a lot of new information to take in; but like any new discipline, it can all be gradually mastered as it becomes more familiar.

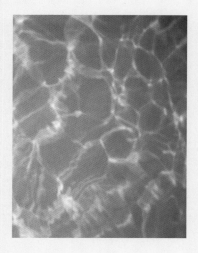

All the techniques you have learned so far have great value. Breath-counting and candle-gazing practices help to center the mind within and still the constant stream of bubbling thoughts. Their main purpose has been to teach you to focus your mind upon one thing at a time.

Pranayama breathing techniques cleanse the mind and emotions. No one would drink dirty water. First, you would throw out the dirty water, clean the glass, and fill it with fresh, clean water. Prana is the fresh water that fills the glass of the mind, replacing the stale and stagnant waters of intruding negative thoughts and emotions. Pranayama is an important practice because you cannot meditate well and experience bliss if the mind and the emotional nature are full of junk. Clear out the clutter first, and then peace will come of itself. Use pranayama as a method of garbage clearance on all levels. Remember that pranayama will cleanse, heal, and strengthen the physical as well as the spiritual body.

Whether it is accepted by some readers or not, sounding the AUM mantra in the energy centers or chakras of the body really does invigorate at subtle levels. This is also a deeply purifying technique and is, if you like, a spiritual tonic. AUM is also a great point of focus.

All these techniques are training you to have a mind focused on one point, to cleanse the mind and emotions of negativity, and to bring in spiritual energy. With regular practice and discipline, you will begin to feel the subtle effects of spiritual energy at work via its agent, prana. As you proceed on your journey, you will discover these truths for yourself.

The meditator is on a mysterious journey, like the caver who travels to the bowels of the Earth, and each individual discovers his or her own realities, although there are many experiences common to all. And it is the joy of these discoveries and experiences that is the reward for your diligent practice.

EXPERIENCES OF MEDITATION

One of the experiences of meditation is to see lights, particularly tiny, bright pinpoint lights, even though the eyes may be closed. You may have visions of people's faces appearing upon the screen of the mind, sometimes kindly and benevolent, sometimes nasty and ugly. But even the most unsavory faces cannot harm you. If you see anything unpleasant at all, in whatever guise it may take, try to cultivate a detached point of view and do not be afraid. You can mentally tell anything unpleasant to go away and it will. These insubstantial images have no substance or actual power to harm you. They arise to "test your mettle" especially when you first begin to sit for meditation. These visions form part of the tricks that your lower self tries to play in an attempt to dissuade your higher Self from seeking progress upon the spiritual path. The lower self is fearful of personal and spiritual development and is daring you to give up. Cast fear aside, for it has no place in meditation.

Other visions during meditation may be very beautiful, such as wonderful natural scenes or even cities, palaces, and temples. Enjoy these and use them as a point of focus for meditation and contemplation. Sometimes you will see Buddhas or Christ-like images, which can be very uplifting. Enjoy them and be grateful they have entered into your consciousness. Often beautiful visions are accompanied by inspiring spiritual feelings. Absorb this beauty, both visually and spiritually, and let the energy that arises from the experience fill you. It is a delight, and everyday earthly experiences are but shadows in comparison.

THE GOAL OF MEDITATION

Enjoy your visions, accept them for what they stimulate within you, and be especially appreciative when they uplift and encourage you in your efforts to go within the Self. Nevertheless, bear in mind that all these wonderful visions and experiences are not the actual goal of meditation itself. We are not meditating in

order to just enjoy a spiritual "trip." (However, it is a better and healthier trip than that produced by other means, such as drugs for example.) The enjoyment of the meditative state is a pleasant reward but still not the goal.

The goal of meditation is, in part, whatever you choose to make of it. We all have our own personal motivations for meditating, and each of us seeks a personal end. That end may be just to wind down at the close of a hard day's work, or perhaps to attain a little more peace of mind in each day's activities. Perhaps you are hoping to calm the bubbling thoughts in order to sleep better at night, learning how to shut down the mind. Maybe through meditation you are training yourself to still the emotions, to let go of past traumas, old fears, anger, resentment, or bitterness, all of which can remain locked up inside and hold you back from living life more constructively. Maybe you wish to develop greater powers of concentration for studying or to improve athletic abilities by training the mind to be focused on one point. You may wish to use it to relax the mind at the end of the day. All of these goals are valid reasons for taking up meditation, and there are many more reasons why people meditate. A very nice young woman who attends my meditation classes initially came along in order to recover from personal bereavement. Her fiancé was tragically killed in a car crash, and, needless to say, she came to the class feeling very down indeed. Yet, after just 5 months of meditation, her spirits had lifted enormously, even though it was only a year since her loss. She is now a much happier, more content person. She tells me enthusiastically that she ascribes this uplifted feeling to meditation. We see in this wonderful example the far-reaching effects of going inward and healing ourselves through that inner, still space within.

Beyond all our personal reasons for meditating, the most important motive should be a spiritual yearning. Some people do not have this spiritual aspiration, but in my experience as a teacher of meditation, many do. Often meditation itself, no matter why it was undertaken, leads to a search for more meaning in our lives and from that a spiritual motive begins to emerge.

HOW MEDITATION CAN BECOME SPIRITUAL

It is important to bring the mind and emotions under control. By stilling the unnecessary thoughts and the negative emotions that cloud judgment, you are consciously engaged in your own personal evolution. You are consciously taking charge of yourself, that is, taking charge of the lesser part of you—the mind and emotions—and thinking and feeling from the standpoint of the higher Self or soul. The thoughts that arise in your mind and the feelings that arise in your emotions are not in reality coming from you. This is a revolutionary statement, but I believe it is a true statement. Your real Self, the true you, is not the physical body with all its imperfections or the emotional nature with all of its various changing states; neither

is it the mind with all its constant streams of jumbled and disconnected thoughts. Your body digests and gets tired and hungry and needs sleep and you have little control over any of that. This is not *you*. The physical body operates quite separately from the real you. The emotional nature isn't you either. Think of those times when you felt hurt, lost and lonely, offended, angry, or desirous of something and later looked back and wondered why you ever felt such a way or why you ever desired this or that. Think of all those things that you once desired and then having experienced them or having lost or failed to attain them, they have disappeared from the forefront of your consciousness. The emotions and feelings associated with these desired objects dissolved away; they are as nebulous and airy as smoke on the wind. We are not our changeable emotions and desires. Meditation shows us that.

To some extent we can get nearer to the real Self through the pathway of the mind. But the mind body is not unlike the emotional body. The mind is also changeable and, like the emotions, deceives us with fresh delights and interests. It is easy to accept that the physical body is only an overcoat or sheath and that the emotional nature is but another body, differing only in that its substance is finer than that of the physical body. But remember, the mind body is also a sheath, of yet finer substance, and yet this is still not the real Self, the In-dweller within us. We are more than the sum of our parts, more than our physical body, our emotions, or our mind. Think of all the unwanted thoughts that drift into our consciousness throughout any one day. How many times do we create mind images of how we want to be, only to change those images at a later date? How many times do we hold one view of ourselves in mind, only to find that others perceive us quite differently. Are we really in control of these thoughts and images any more than we are in control of physical sensations or needs such as hunger or sleep? The mind has its own workings, and they are often contrary to the inner Self. But the process of meditation teaches us to use the mind to control the emotions and even the physical body. After you are experienced in meditation, the mind becomes more potent, and mental images of yourself become stronger and more positive and will be perceived as such by others. Of all the three lesser bodies— the physical, emotional, and mental—it is the mental vehicle that will ultimately

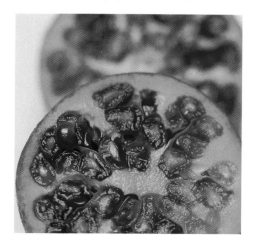

become your best friend. Control the mind and make it your servant, and it will be constantly faithful to you, governing the turbulent and unpredictable emotions and the heavy, unreliable, and lazy body. Yet remember that even the mind is not the Self. The true Self is the spiritual energy within, the core of your being. It is that Self that aspires toward spiritual things. It is the center where the stillness is found and known. Meditation is the key to that Self, the soul within.

WHAT IS THE STILLNESS?

Most people are always actively seeking something,
desiring material things, such as more money, a better
house, or a newer car. This may be all right in itself, but if
we allow these desires to overtake us and become
swamped with anxiety, we become deluded, negative
individuals. We have to know when enough is enough, and
learn to become more content within. Only in the quiet of
the heart and mind is real peace from the troubles and
worries of the world ever found.

It is difficult to describe the stillness within because it
has to be entered into naturally, like falling asleep. No
one ever tries to go to sleep, for if you try, it does not
occur. Sleep is entered into by simply letting it happen.
You cannot make sleep happen. The stillness within, the
state of true meditation, is the same, except that you
will be more fully conscious than when you are in normal
waking consciousness. This is where meditation differs
from sleep. In sleep, consciousness is diminished; in
meditation, it is enhanced.

The stillness may be described as a point of no thought.
In this state, you will find that all the meditational
practices have led you into an altered state that feels
distinctly higher, nobler, and more real than the usual
condition that we take for the norm. We are only half
awake compared to this altered state, and there is no
ordinary everyday comparison.

You find yourself entering a state of stillness, but you do not do it consciously. In this state, the breath is virtually nonexistent and suspended, and the thoughts have ceased altogether. The emotions are forgotten completely. This is the point of stillness. The physical body is absolutely still, the emotions are quelled, and the mind is perfectly thoughtless. A balance exists on all three planes.

In such a poised condition, sensations arise from soul levels, bringing feelings of bliss and divine rapture. You may perhaps see visions. Whatever you see, or do not see, you will be pervaded by a feeling of benevolence, of being present within an energy that can only be described as the highest love. It is not an emotional love but a divine, detached, yet all-inclusive love; it is an inner radiance that seems to come from your own true Self, the soul.

I could elaborate at length, but still I would not adequately describe this experience. It is a journey deep within the cave of the inner Self, and this discovery is a rich treasure of gems that makes every step of the journey worth it.

The joy and bliss that derive from finding the stillness within may even bring tears to your eyes, but again, they are not attended with strong emotion and sobbing. The tears are ecstatic and just roll down from a perfectly composed face. Often the hairs on your arms will stand up, and you may have goose bumps. This is not a frightening experience; but it is part of the sensation of entering into a higher state of being. There is never any fear in this experience; on the contrary, one feels bathed in light and perfection.

SAMADHI

This type of deep stillness is also known as Samadhi, which is the Sanskrit for "superconsciousness." This word describes the condition most adequately. Super-consciousness—in other words, *above* consciousness. You have risen above the threshold of normal Earthly consciousness and have touched the realm of the true Self, the soul. All knowledge is found here, and you will return with greater wisdom and love, although this may not be obvious at first. When you enter Samadhi you will learn much in this state, most of which will filter into your life in subtle ways. I will say no more, for the stillness of Samadhi must become your own truth, not mine.

One final word, after tantalizing you with the hope of reaching this goal. The point of absolute stillness, of no-thought, of Samadhi itself, is not easy to obtain. Without wishing to sound sanctimonious, one must become worthy of this experience. Meditation and improving the way we live our lives and how we deal with others teaches us to become worthy. But, bear in mind that although Samadhi is not easy to attain, it is not impossible. Many have experienced it, including myself. If it were not so, no one would have ever heard of it.

8: NONATTACHMENT, ILLUSIONS, AND VIRTUES

Meditation is more than just experiencing some kind of personal happiness. Happiness does have a part to play, of course, and for most people the attainment of inner happiness is probably a prime motive in the first place. But the goal of meditation must also surely be about becoming a better person, relating to the world in which we live and to the people around us in a better way.

When we go deep within and examine ourselves, we are often made acutely aware of our shortcomings. Such an awareness should never be avoided. In recognizing our failings, we become determined to change ourselves and to foster the more positive characteristics. In this way, we learn Christ's true meaning when he says "Do unto others as you would have them do unto you." After we have developed true self-awareness, it becomes virtually impossible to cause hurt or offense to anyone because we have the constant consciousness of how it feels to be ill-used in any way. That does not imply that we should allow ourselves to become victims, letting others do as they please with us; it means instead that we will never, ever, be the perpetrators of wrongdoing, be that slander, criticism, physical violence, or cruelty.

Meditation (much of which is concentrated self-inquiry) sensitizes us to those around us, and teaches us to become more all-inclusive in our relations with our fellow human beings. We now find that we watch our words and actions, and even our thoughts come under a higher scrutiny. This happens because we are actively taking part in our own evolution by meditating regularly and endeavoring to carry this meditative state over into everyday affairs. It is just like any training routine such as working out in a gym; at first the results are not seen, but bit by bit, changes are noted, and eventually you cannot leave the practice alone.

NONATTACHMENT

In Eastern philosophy, nonattachment is spoken of frequently. Usually, people associate this attitude of mind with religious ascetics wearing loincloths and living solitary existences in caves, forests, or monasteries. But the state of nonattachment is not confined to those who have shaved their heads and taken vows of celibacy. Indeed, it is possible to be *in* the world but not *of* the world. In fact, it is perhaps a greater measure of your character and spiritual development when you are living in the world, surrounded by every kind of temptation (from objects to modes of behavior), and yet have little or no desire or attachment to these material things.

It is easier to be nonattached if one lives within the confines of a monastery and has few possessions, but real nonattachment is actually having material things yet not feeling inwardly possessive of them, and not desiring more. It is all a state of mind. There are those people who have little and yet are greedy and selfish with the little they have. Poverty of itself is not a virtue, although some philosophies will have you think that it is so. On the other hand, some individuals have great wealth and yet do not value it greedily, giving away what they can and living mentally detached from their possessions. However, I emphasize that this is rare. For the most part, ownership of possessions tends to bind people to them, which is why the

philosophy of poverty as a virtue has come about. But as with all aspects of life, a more balanced perspective is needed, and in the case of personal possessions it seems that the best approach is to avoid extremes either way. If you are clothed, fed, and housed and if your earnings exceed your expenses, you are probably happy, having enough to be comfortable. Obviously, living in this world of constant financial demands may put pressure upon you to earn more and so improve your lot in life. Most of us are under this kind of pressure; few of us want to live in the poorer high-crime areas, or in dismal high-rise apartment buildings. In order to escape unsatisfactory environments we must be able to afford to live somewhere that is conducive to our inner peace, physical security, and happiness. But people often forget themselves and continue to desire more than they could really need, and so disturb their peace of mind with constant nagging desires to acquire more.

From a spiritual perspective, money is not evil in itself, and neither is it wrong to be rich. For example, a penniless beggar may have more greed in his heart than a wealthy businessman who supports charities anonymously and generously. Try to see money and possessions as a form of energy to be used wisely, not just for ourselves, but ultimately for the good of all.

Nonattachment to anything that we consider "ours," whether that be money, property, or even loved ones, brings peace of mind. It is our possessiveness that causes the emotional and mental disturbance. Possessiveness can destroy marriages if partners desire to own each other. The reality is that none of us owns anything, we merely borrow and use things during our lifetime. Many of our financial interactions are illusory. For example, we use checks or credit cards to pay for things, or to cover our debts and mortgages, without any actual visible cash changing hands. All these financial transactions are but figures printed on paper; real currency is rarely seen by anyone. So in many respects, finances are but an illusion, and a very powerful one indeed. You might wish to meditate on this subject.

When the constant nagging desires become subdued, we find ourselves becoming released inwardly from what has felt like a prison. When this is experienced, it becomes obvious that it is attachment to possessions that binds us. When we break the shackles of attachment, there comes an exhilarating and liberating freedom that brings a growing tranquility to our whole nature.

We become attached to many things in the course of our lives, not just money and material possessions. We form painful bonds to other people, becoming mentally and emotionally intoxicated and addicted as if to a drug. We may foolishly love the wrong person and even make ourselves sick over such attachments, becoming truly "lovesick." Then, when the veil of illusion is lifted, we look back and marvel that we could have even been attracted to that person in the first place! We spend a lot of time fooling ourselves, and all of this because of our desire for attachment. Regular meditation gradually loosens our bonds of attachment to the things of this world, whether those bonds are material, emotional, or mental. You will recognize your own bonds and eliminate them over time, and simultaneously you will refine your healthier connections to things and to people. You will learn to cultivate a paradoxical viewpoint that acknowledges the value of material objects yet does not have an attitude of ownership toward those objects. You will still love friends and family as before, but operating from this more advanced perspective you will be able to stand back from them in a nonpossessive way. This will not diminish your natural feelings, but will actually deepen them. Your love relationships of all kinds will allow the other person to be free to be him- or herself, and any sense of ownership or proprietorship over those you love, or think you love, will gradually dissolve. This is detachment. It will not make you cold, hard, or clinical; it will merely remove the illusions that bind. Experience will teach you what this means.

We may not realize how our attachment to objects and to other people impedes our fine-tuning as human beings. For example, a surgeon must cultivate nonattachment in order to perform complicated operations successfully. Personal attachment to the patient could cloud the mind and interfere with the surgeon's judgment. Our daily attachments are very powerful influences.

ILLUSIONS

The world around us is full of illusions. These illusions are the result of identification with the physical body, the emotions, and thoughts. Many people think that they are basically the physical body, that the billions of cells that make up the body is the sum total of the person. But this is not true.

You are not your physical body, you only inhabit it. It is a scientific fact that within every seven years all of the cells in your body have changed, even the bone cells. The physical body you inhabit now is not the same body you identified with seven years ago. It merely follows the same genetic structure, and the present cells are only copies of those that existed previously. Yet amid all this physical transformation, your consciousness remains the same; your consciousness—not your physical body—comprises the real you.

You are not the physical body any more than you are the clothes you are wearing. Your clothes only appear to have animated motion when you move or walk because of the action of your body moving or walking, but after you shed those clothes they fall into a lifeless heap. Nevertheless people are often attracted to people because of the clothes they are wearing, and all of us are judged by the garments we wear. A smart suit gets a very different reaction from people than does a pair of dirty overalls. People often see the outer covering only and mistake that for who we are; in many instances, we ourselves change character in order to match our outfit.

There are many parallels between the nature of clothes and the nature of the physical body. Just as the clothes we wear are animated by our physical movements, having no inherent life of their own, so, in like manner, our physical bodies are also animated only by the presence of soul energy. If the real you, the soul, withdraws from the body, it too, like the clothes you discard, will fall into a lifeless heap. Remember that you are not this body, but the in-dweller within the outer shell. The body has no life without the real you to animate it.

Maybe all of this seems far-fetched, but let me give you an example of a very real experience that I had when I was not much more than 18 months old. I was sitting in the garden of my parents' home wearing a cotton diaper. The sun was bright and warm and my little baby hand was quite happily scooping up bare soil and stuffing it into my mouth. I can still remember the earthy taste of the soil and even the slight grittiness of its texture upon my infant gums, tongue, and palate. I could feel the crunch of the soil in my little mouth. I can see clearly, even now as I write, my small, pudgy baby hands and rounded baby belly. I remember as clearly as if it were yesterday, rubbing the soil on my belly and scooping up more soil to eat.

You may be thinking that this childhood memory is not so remarkable, or at least it is only remarkable in the sense that the memory is so vivid at such a young age. That, and no more. But this was not the end of the experience. There was something else that happened, something more real and distinct than merely the experience of eating soil: I felt much *older* than the body I was in, as if I was upon another plane or higher level than that of the physical, infant body that mechanically ate soil like an automaton. I felt that the baby was not *me*, at least not entirely me. I could feel that I was already knowledgeable and perhaps, to a degree, evolved. There was a strong feeling of being distinctly separate from the baby form, and I felt that I was attempting to "get to grips" with the mechanism of my new body, trying to control its automatonlike behavior. I was, in that moment, aware of being distinctly another presence, a being that was higher, older, and from another plane of consciousness. *That* is the remarkable aspect of this experience. I had a clear impression that I was much more than my physical body.

You may think that this is incredible, or even fanciful. You can draw your own conclusions. But it doesn't end there. One of my older brothers (who would have been only about 10 years old at the time) saw the baby me sitting in the garden and called out to my mother, who was inside the house, "Stevie's eating dirt again!" He then promptly came into the garden and picked me up. I recall being held in his arms and he was talking to me, asking me what I was doing eating dirt. But by this point, the magic had been broken, and I have no more recollection regarding this incident beyond the point where I was lifted up into my brother's arms. Yet how could I have understood his words at that age? Word for word, I remember exactly what he said when he called out to my mother as quoted above. Do 18-month-old babies really know, and remember, the words that are said to them? I wonder.

This experience highlights the continuity of consciousness, at least as far as I am concerned. I was already a conscious, aware entity, dwelling upon a plane outside physical consciousness. This precious experience has never left me, and I think of it from time to time as a source of comfort in an often hard and seemingly meaningless world. What this experience reveals is that the soul exists in its own plane or dimension. I was often reminded of this experience as I grew up, several times being suddenly and quite unexpectedly overshadowed by the peculiar sensation that I was not this body, not this little self, but another Self. Even at eight or nine years old I can distinctly remember my own words to one of my brothers, when I asked him if he had similar experiences (which he did not, incidentally), telling him that I felt as if "I am me, and yet I am not me." Poignant words for a child of such an age.

The truth is, we identify with the physical body when in fact it serves only as a vehicle of expression for the true Self who dwells upon a higher level. People are constantly identifying with other things as well. They buy the latest high-tech car, for instance, and when driving it they think the car is somehow an extension of the Self. In a sense, it becomes so, and other people who are also blinded by the love of material things believe it to be so as well and then associate the individual with a Porsche or a Mercedes. Isn't it ridiculous? If people play this attachment and identification game with a mechanical lump of painted metal, then how much more will they identify and be attached to their own physical bodies? They even identify with the physical body when they are dissatisfied with it. Such is the bond and the illusion of matter.

People extend this identification toward a great many other aspects, pertaining to their personal experiences. We do this in our working field, when we accept a label that calls us "painter and decorator," "nurse," "accountant," or "unemployed." Call someone a name often

enough and she believes it. Anyone who has been labeled as "stupid" or "useless" all of his or her life will end up believing it. Place anyone in any working environment and it isn't long before he or she is speaking and behaving in a manner that typifies someone who does that particular job. Doctors usually speak to their patients in a certain characteristic way; truck drivers chat to their workmates in a way that fits in with their job;

bankers behave and speak in ways that are unique to their profession; clerics adopt their own peculiar characteristics that befit their calling. Everyone begins to play a part, acting out behavior that is, largely speaking, expected of them. All of us are players upon the stage of life, just as Shakespeare said. The man who is called "bank manager" will wear his neat suit and try to speak politely yet authoritatively, attempting to give an air of personal affluence even though the money he is entrusted to lend you belongs to the investors in the bank and doesn't actually come from his own personal fortune! The roadworker who is covered with mud all day long may be a first-rate

human being, but the very nature of his job will often make him adopt a coarse demeanor in order to suit the environment in which he finds himself. You can observe this in all walks of life; all of us are merely acting out roles, and in many respects, doing exactly what others expect of us. In this way, we identify with our mental and emotional fields of expression and believe ourselves to be the person the label says we are. We end up believing the insults we receive, and, if we're lucky, the praise too. We tread a fine line in what we accept as our reality and must balance this with our own inner wisdom. Others will often convince us of the truth of their version of reality, no matter how unjust or untruthful. Look at the influence of Adolf Hitler, how his own distorted personality swept a whole nation into an emotional furor and made them shriek "Sieg Heil!," raising their right arms to the Führer and giving themselves over to support his call.

Each person reading this book will recall personal examples of people who gossip in the workplace. They find a victim and repeat bits of information that they have heard about the person second-hand. In the end they are believing lies. They then encourage you to do likewise. In a sense, that is what has happened in this world of illusion. Truth is distorted, and the distortion is elaborated upon until we are all believing a pack of lies. You have been told that you are your body, and because everyone else seems to think that this is true, then so do you. Before long, the truth has been lost altogether.

The emotional world of feeling is as illusory as the physical world; it is no more a part of the real Self than the physical body is. It, too, is full of falsehood and broken dreams and will never bring fulfillment. Meditation teaches us to step outside our distorted emotions and see things as they really are, like waking from a bad dream; while dreaming the images seem real, but upon waking, they are seen for what they really are—nothing but a dream.

Everyone is looking for happiness in the material, emotional, and mental world in one way or another. People may try to find it through acquiring possessions or finding romance or by passing exams and attaining professional qualifications. In countless ways people look for fulfillment and happiness. All of these things have their place, of course, and can all be used to gain experience of life, but it is our attachment to them that must change.

We fool ourselves mentally all the time by saying such things as "I am a secretary" or a "college don," or that I am "rich" or "poor." Although these terms serve to describe a current situation at a certain point in our lives, we must remember that all such situations are temporary and do not describe the bigger picture of an individual. They are merely labels that identify our position and status at a particular point in our life's drama. If you continuously believe a label, you mentally reinforce it and then restrict the opportunity for going beyond it. You become identified with the illusion and forgetful of your true nature.

We are surrounded then by three great illusions: the physical body, the emotional world, and the mental realm. These three illusory states constitute the three aspects of a person's personality—the body, the emotions, and the mind. They are like three wild horses that are out of control. You must attach these wild animals to the chariot of the soul in order to bring them under control and drive them toward your goal. Your true Self acts as the charioteer, and only that Self can guide the three wild horses of the personality, bringing them under control and ultimately transcending them. When you have tamed the three wild horses your life will be guided by your higher Self.

I am not saying that transcending the personality is going to be easy, but I do know that if you are serious about your spiritual progress, you will never find fulfillment or happiness in the three lower worlds. Happiness can be found only within the Self, by discovering the light that shines therein.

THE VIRTUES

No progress can be expected in meditation if you are not trying to develop your character. If meditation is geared toward acquiring psychic faculties (that are often a natural outcome) and is centered solely on a variety of selfish interests, then you cannot expect much real progress. To obtain the very best from your meditations, you must strive to unfold all the latent qualities in your nature, specifically those qualities that lie dormant and unexpressed. For example, if you know in yourself that you are not very courageous and have a reticent, timid personality, then you may go into your meditations and dwell on aspects of courage, such as heroism, sacrifice, strength of character, and the ability to stand by your own understanding of truth. Another good idea is to read inspiring books about real-life heroic acts and meditate upon them. Or you can listen to music that has heroic connotations to inspire this characteristic within yourself. In time, you will actually *have* more courage, for the power of the contemplative mind is immense.

If you find giving and loving a difficulty, then you can meditate upon love in all its forms. Dwell upon the loving deeds of Jesus Christ, for example, or Mother Teresa, or

anyone else whom you may personally know who displays loving characteristics. By thinking about others who love deeply, you also will tap into that same pool of love from which they gain their inspiration and will soon begin to incorporate similar characteristics into your own nature. Eventually, the love nature will unfold and reveal itself in your character.

During meditation we can all tap into an invisible energy pool and draw out the virtues we need by focusing our minds and willing ourselves to express those virtues. If wisdom seems lacking, you can meditate upon wisdom, and particularly upon those whom you know to be wise; think of the Buddha, for example, or Gandhi, or anyone else you consider to be wise. Dwell upon all the benefits of living wisely, and before long, wisdom shall be yours. Tap into the universal pool of wisdom when you meditate, and, because wisdom already lies hidden within you, it will unfold and reveal itself.

Maybe you have trouble with honesty. Perhaps speaking the truth does not come easily to you. Meditate upon truth and what that means to you, not just in the sense of speaking truthfully as best you know, but in living as a truthful being. In other words, meditate upon becoming the truth that you talk about to others. Be an example of that truth.

There are many virtues, and by meditating upon them and their qualities, you may acquire them bit by bit.

VIVEKA AND VAIRAGYA

Viveka **and** *vairagya* **are the Sanskrit words** for
discrimination and dispassion.

Viveka, or discrimination, is the ability to dispel illusions
by discerning rightly between the real and the unreal,
between the Self or soul and the not-Self. This means
recognizing the difference between that which is
permanent and that which is impermanent, valuing
that which is eternal, enduring, and consequently
spiritually beneficial, over the transient impermanence
of material goods and all the things that cannot last.
The mystical, spiritual values will always endure, even
when all else in the world fails and disappoints. By
developing discrimination, we become "disillusioned"
with the transitory world. At first, disillusionment seems
painful, but it is followed by a great sense of relief and
peace. Discrimination is an excellent tool for breaking
the spell of illusion.

Vairagya, or dispassion, is very closely related to
discrimination. It is the ability to stand back from the
emotions and to see things clearly and with
nonattachment, watching the play of the emotions
carefully, but not becoming entangled. The emotions
act like alcohol, dulling the senses. A dispassionate
approach to life helps us to see things with a clear
head and to make appropriate and wise decisions.

Dispassion does not turn us into cold, calculating machines, rather it helps us to see the greater picture in any situation. It does not imply that our ability to love is compromised in any way. But it does mean that our love-nature is wiser. When meditating, allow the mind to dwell upon the nature of dispassion, and you will develop this quality of sublime detachment.

Dispassion must also be extended toward ourselves; we have to learn to stand back from our own pain and suffering and not wallow in self-pity. Self-pity is most destructive and can lead to depression. We must view life and all its sorrows with nonattachment, view them dispassionately as mere illusions. It is not easy, but when dispassion is applied to all things and in every circumstance, you will be released from suffering. It is only our attachment to things that causes misery. Think on this.

9: what to expect from meditation

The regular practice of meditation will not transform you into a perfect person, but it may give you a greater degree of peace of mind and a happier, more reflective outlook on life. Sometimes, the results of meditation are enormous and life-changing, as they have been in my own personal life. Believe me, I am a long way from being perfect, but I do know that without meditation in my life I would be much less of a person than I am today.

So what should you expect from meditation? Well, you should not actually be looking for results per se. You should engage in meditation for its own sake rather than with a particular goal in mind. If you follow the meditational practice regularly and enjoy it, the results will come naturally of themselves. The secret of success in meditation is to absolutely love it!

However, there are many benefits for the serious meditator. On a physical level you will slow down the aging process, because meditation slows the pulse and heart rate, and thus reduces the risk of strokes and heart attacks, lowers the effects of cholesterol, and reduces the harm caused by a multitude of toxic substances in the bloodstream. Experienced meditators often develop very lustrous eyes and a healthy glow to the skin as a result of pranayama exercises, sounding the AUM, and directing prana through the chakras. Meditators tend to need less sleep and awaken more refreshed. On an emotional level, as you become an experienced meditator you will probably gain more poise and control, handling stressful situations with a greater degree of tolerance and patience. This is where the virtues come in, particularly the qualities of discrimination and dispassion. Your relationships with others should improve vastly, and you will find that as you become calmer and more "at one" with yourself, this feeling will radiate magnetically from within you, reaching out toward

others. They will sense this subconsciously, and respond positively to you. An experienced meditator does tend to radiate an inner calm and sense of harmlessness that cannot help but influence others in a positive way, unless they happen to be extremely violent or cruel. This harmlessness is not the result of weakness or cowardliness but of the desire not to harm anyone or anything. The meditator

becomes benevolent to all other living creatures and has their well-being at heart. In Sanskrit, this quality is known as *ahimsa* and means noninjury in thought, word, and deed.

To live one's life according to practices of benevolence and empathy is not a sign of weakness, rather, it takes enormous strength of character and courage. When confronted by a person living in a state of ahimsa, the average reasonable person will feel uplifted, and his or her anger or sense of hopelessness and unhappiness will simply vanish into thin air.

As your meditation practices continue, you should discover that you know yourself more fully and deeply, making the right decisions for the real you instead of choosing unsatisfactory conditions that are the cause of your unrest. Gradually, your life's direction seems to take a new and better turn, and your willpower and strength of mind increases. You think things through more carefully, taking measured thought instead of reacting from emotional gutfeelings that are often deceptive because they are usually the result of negative emotions such as fear, anger, or desperation. The intuitive faculty, which comes from the higher Self or soul and which gives us the wisest answers to life's problems, will become stronger and guide you in a more positive direction.

INTUITION

Intuition comes with the unfolding of our spiritual potential. Intuition—what is the meaning of this word? When we break it down we have "in-tuition," in other words, "inner learning." We are being taught from within. It is our inner tuition.

This inner learning can only be accessed by coming into contact with our true Self, or soul. It is essentially a spiritual energy that we are learning to contact through the meditation experience.

Because of your regular practice in meditation, you will find that you have a greater enthusiasm for life, even though you are in fact going inward and withdrawing from the outer life. This is yet another paradox of meditation. Although you may have less interest in the outer material world in some respects, you will at the same time develop a very powerful and enthusiastic interest in deeper matters and, as a result, your ordinary, everyday affairs will be enhanced. You will concentrate better, even upon that which you might have previously considered to be boring tasks.

Contacting the intuitive faculty changes your perception of many things. Ideas will seem to "come out of the blue" and you will often feel inspired. These intuitive responses always feel markedly different from gutfeelings, which are merely a reaction to stress.

As your intuition unfolds, you may even experience what might be described as natural highs during the course of the day. Your Crown Chakra may feel energized and open, and you may feel tingling sensations around your arms, neck, and head. These tinglings indicate that you are beginning to sense your own auric space, for one of the results of meditation is an increased awareness and sensitivity to subtle energies. This new awareness will make you feel that your energy bodies have expanded beyond their normal state. This is a beautiful experience, and in this heightened state of awareness you will feel that you are being wafted by an energy that can only be described as benevolent love. It is not an emotionally based love; it is spiritual in quality. It must be experienced to be understood. It must also be treasured when it comes, and the more you meditate, the more frequently will this experience come to you. You will feel wonderful and find that this feeling enhances all that you do and all your interactions with others.

As your intuition grows, you may even have prophetic dreams and during waking consciousness have knowledge of future events. You may even find that your

intuition warns you of danger and prevents you from making wrong choices. Because the energy of the intuition is coming from the soul, it teaches us to be more loving and less selfish, bringing enormous serenity. Life takes on new meaning as we participate in our evolutionary development, filling us with a great inner joy. The effects of meditational practice have spilled over into everyday life. Meditation is, in fact, a continuum; it is not limited to the half hour of sitting. The secret is to keep the energy flowing deep within us throughout the day in all circumstances. Once again, I shall remind you that meditational practices are not easy, but the results are more than worth the effort. We can face life more positively, and instead of collapsing under stress and wailing about our lot in life, we apply our intuition and seek solutions, because now the emotions, which have probably caused us all the trouble in the first place, are more stable, and the mind is stronger and more focused.

EXTRASENSORY PERCEPTION (ESP)

While it should be remembered that the goal of meditation is to make us better beings, it cannot be ignored that the very practice and nature of meditation does open the mind to various psychic influences. Some people are more psychic or attuned to the mystical realms than others. For example, some people are naturally clairvoyant (the psychic ability to perceive subtle visual phenomena beyond the normal range of vision), or clairaudient (the psychic ability to perceive subtle sounds beyond the normal range of hearing), or, as in my case, clairsentient (the psychic ability to sense subtle phenomena such as changes in the atmosphere or energy fields around us). Very often people have a mixture of all these gifts. Most people are actually far more psychic than they realize or will admit. Meditation will often enhance any conscious mystical abilities and can bring latent faculties to the surface. Nonetheless, I cannot emphasize enough that these abilities are not the goal, and that meditation should not be used simply as a tool to develop psychic powers. In the East, the lesser psychic ability is known as a *siddhi*. The siddhis are not regarded as being of any real spiritual value, and in fact are considered to be a possible hindrance

upon the spiritual path. These abilities can make you self-absorbed and distract you from higher, more spiritual goals. There have been many people who are what are commonly known as psychics but very few individuals who are truly spiritual. Relatively speaking, it is fairly easy to be psychic compared to the more difficult task of becoming spiritual.

But, having said all that, I personally feel that psychic powers can also be a great boon to life, both for the individual and for the benefit of others. As long as you don't allow yourself to become obsessed with these abilities, they are perfectly acceptable, and indeed may be a blessing. There are countless cases of people who have saved their own lives and the lives of others by using their psychic powers. There are instances of people being warned not to take a certain flight and the plane has subsequently crashed, or not to go to places where a natural disaster is about to occur, all because they were attuned to their psychic nature. Even on a more mundane and non life-threatening level, people have been given excellent psychically channeled advice that has changed their fortune for the better or provided comfort during a difficult time. We should, therefore, not discount our psychic abilities as unimportant, even if they are derisively called siddhis in Eastern philosophy.

In fact, although many Eastern and Western teachers consider that the siddhis are of a lower order, the Sanskrit word does not merely stand for "psychic power" but also for "perfection." Another esoteric paradox. What really matters is maintaining a sense of balance toward our innate abilities. We should not become egotistical about them, but be grateful for having them, and if we believe in God, thank that Divine Being (using whatever name you wish to ascribe to that Being) for giving us such gifts. If you have such psychic powers, always use them for the greater good, never for selfish motives. There can be a heavy spiritual penalty for the misuse of psychic powers, for such abilities entail a great deal of responsibility; all of our abilities are meant to serve the highest good.

It is important not to become too engrossed in psychic abilities, but simply to acknowledge them and use them wisely. The development of such faculties should not become the prime motive for sitting for meditation. If this occurs, you must recognize this tendency as a trap, for the siddhis can at times become so absorbing that they overshadow character and soul development. Remember, psychic abilities will naturally unfold, so be accepting of them. Just watch the little ego and remind yourself that although you may at times touch upon the Divine within you, you are at the same time human with human faults. The ego, if it arises, can be a monster, and it will assert itself over all reason and attempt to destroy all of your purer motives and intentions. There are many examples of failed gurus who have allowed the petty, egotistical self to take control because their psychic powers have made them proud and arrogant. I personally have witnessed such a demise in certain individuals who shall remain nameless—one in particular was prominent in worldwide esoteric circles and wrote extensively upon subjects relating to the inner world.

It is a sad and pathetic spectacle to witness a highly intelligent and widely educated person fall into the trap of the little selfish ego, simply because he or she has attained a few siddhis and has therefore become a focus of attention. There are many who crave power and too few among us who would really not abuse it. It is a sad reflection upon the human condition that most of those who hold power of any kind do so because they have pursued it for selfish ends rather than to better serve humankind and the world in which we live. Psychic powers carry with them no less a responsibility than do political or financial power, for after we achieve anything that sets us above others in any way, it is our duty to share what we have with the world rather than to use these gifts for self-aggrandizement.

Psychic powers or siddhis will come, which is fine; however, they need to be handled wisely, guided by a loving heart and unselfish character. If you follow this advice, all will be well. If not, do not expect any real spiritual progress.

ENLIGHTENMENT

Meditation gradually dispels illusion. Through meditation, we begin to touch a deeper part of ourself and slowly transcend the lesser, egotistical self with all its cares, worries, and ambitions. We become enlightened. That means that instead of living in the darkness of the little "I" we enter into the light of the true Self. Hence, we become "enlightened." Only in the light can one truly see. Most people, however, live in darkness and are ignorant of the great well of truth that lies within. It is as if, to return to our caver analogy, they are stumbling around in the realms of the inner Self without a lantern to light the way. All around them lies the rich treasure of the Self—those gem-encrusted rocks—but they cannot see what is within their very grasp. Only by going within the Self and seeking the truth that lies there, with wisdom and love in the heart, can light be finally shed upon us.

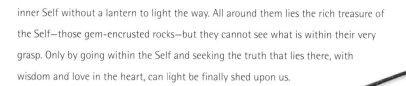

These words may seem esoteric and obscure, and perhaps they do not make sense for you. That is inevitable, for you must do your own searching and arrive at your own understanding. In the words of Christ; "Seek and you shall find, ask and you shall receive, knock and the door shall be opened to you."

In all your developmental and meditational practices, cultivate patience. If you are too eager and attempt to rush, you will become agitated, and real growth will be stunted. Consider the mighty oak tree. At first, a sapling oak is unnoticed and insignificant, and for a long, long time it grows in a slow, unobtrusive manner. Yet it is slow but sure. Little spring flowers may come up quickly and look delightful, but they are here today and gone tomorrow. The oak endures. Ultimately it stands the test of time and becomes a haven for birds and gives shelter. The oak provides a majestic symbol of the wise growth of the soul and has all the qualities that one would expect from spiritual evolution: strength, steadiness, endurance, abundance, majesty, and beauty.

As spiritual beings, we are seeking the kind of growth that endures. With a slow, steady, and plodding growth, we endure and become stronger in our development, putting down long and deep tap roots that anchor us in our true nature.

Your true nature is the soul. It is a center of love, wisdom, and bliss. Everything that I have attempted to teach you in this book has been geared toward helping you understand that meditation is the master key that unlocks the door to the soul.

appendix

EASY REFERENCE OF TECHNIQUES

This final chapter is to be used as a quick reference section so that you can easily follow the techniques of meditation outlined throughout this book.

PREPARATION

1. Select a convenient time and place to meditate, and try to stick to this time each day if possible. I recommend first thing in morning as it helps many people conduct the rest of the day calmly and with focus.

2. Set a soft-toned alarm before you, timing for at least 10 minutes and up to half an hour.

3. An excellent idea is to play some music that inspires you and helps to create the meditative mood. You will know yourself what to select for this purpose. Music is not compulsory; it is a matter of personal choice. The accompanying CD has suitable music. However, you may prefer absolute silence.

4. **Wear loose clothing,** dim the lights, close the drapes, take the phone off the hook, etc.

5. Make sure that you are sitting comfortably, either in a chair or on the floor cross-legged, or in the Lotus position if you are able.

THE CONCENTRATION PRACTICES

BREATH COUNTING

1. Close your eyes. Begin by focusing on the breath, just breathing in and out through the nose in a slow, steady, regular rhythm.

2. Begin mentally to count on every out-breath. On the first out-breath, count "One." On the second out-breath, count "Two." On the third out-breath, count "Three." On the fourth out-breath, count "Four." Complete the cycle again and again until the soft alarm brings the practice to a close.

CANDLE GAZING

This exercise can be practiced using the Meditation CD.

You may use candle gazing instead of breath counting or in succession to it, or even prior to breath counting. You may even do candle gazing while performing breath counting at the same time if you wish. Find a method that suits you.

1. Choose a candle that is pleasing to you.

2. Place the candle in a secure candle holder upon a completely empty table so that you have no other distractions. NEVER LEAVE A CANDLE UNATTENDED.

3. Position a comfortable chair with a straight back before the candle and table insuring that the candle is directly in front of you and preferably at eye level. It should be placed between one and two feet away from your eyes.

4. Light the candle. Turn off other lights, and close the drapes.

5. Set your alarm or begin listening to the CD.

6. Whether you have just done breath counting or not, begin by relaxing with some slow, steady inhalations and exhalations through the nose.

7. Allow the eyes to gaze softly upon the candle flame. The eyes rarely blink, and do not move either up or down or to the side. The eyes become absorbed in softly focusing upon the flame. The breath becomes subdued.

8. The alarm sounds or my voice will bring you round.

9. Now palm the hands gently over the eyes. Do not press upon the eyeballs. Allow the eyes to adjust to the blackness of the palmed hands and watch the afterimage point of light at the center of the mind. Enjoy the color changes that it undergoes; you have earned the pleasure of them.

10. When all the colors have disappeared, take your hands away and bring your practice to a close. Don't forget to blow out the candle .

As you progress in concentration practices you will definitely want to go into a deeper state, and may carry on from candle gazing directly into meditation. Naturally, you will set your alarm accordingly right from the beginning if you have chosen to meditate for, say, half an hour. You will begin to judge quite accurately how long you have been breath counting or candle gazing, and may dispense with timing these practices, or using the CD, as you become more used to them.

BREATH COUNTING WITH RETENTION OF BREATH

1. Begin by regulating the breathing rhythm as in ordinary breath counting.

2. On the first inhalation, mentally count "One" and then hold the breath. Judge for yourself how long the in-breath should be, and how long the retention should be. Don't overtax yourself.

3. Release the breath in a slow, steady, relaxed manner. There is no gasping or sense of panic.

4. Take the second in-breath and count "Two." Hold the breath. Release. Carry on breathing and retaining the breath until the fourth breath. Repeat the cycle of counting from one to four again.

5. Remember that all breathing is via the nostrils.

PURIFICATION TECHNIQUES

DIGITAL PRANAYAMA

This exercise can be practiced using the Meditation CD.

1. Sit either in a comfortable chair without armrests or on the floor on a cushion either cross-legged or in the Half Lotus or Full Lotus.

2. Rest both hands on your knees or in your lap or upper thighs.

3. Take a few regular breaths to begin with, breathing through the nostrils, not the mouth.

4. Raise the right hand to the face. Leave a gap between the armpit and the body.

5. Fold the index, middle, and ring fingers into the palm of the hand (see pages 48-51).

6. Close the right nostril with the thumb.

BEGIN ONE ROUND

7. Breathe in through the left nostril to a count of four seconds.

8. Close the left nostril with the ring and little finger, keeping the thumb closed on the right nostril. Hold the breath to a count of eight seconds.

9. Release the thumb, and breathe out of the right nostril to a count of six seconds.

10. Breathe in the right nostril to a count of four seconds.

11. Close the right nostril with the thumb, keeping the left nostril closed at the same time. Hold the breath again to a count of eight seconds.

12. Release the ring and little fingers from the left nostril to a count of six seconds.

END OF THE ROUND

You may keep a count of rounds by using the fingers of the left hand as outlined on pages 50-51 or by simply setting your alarm and just continuing with digital pranayama until the alarm sounds. If the alarm rings at any point partway through your digital pranayama, always insure that you complete the practice by breathing out of the left nostril so that the round is fully completed. This ends the session neatly.

Remember that you can extend the length of time on the in-breaths, out-breaths, and breath-holding sequences, and on the number of rounds. Be sensible, don't strain, and try to remain patient. The greatest benefits from this method of pranayama will come from maintaining a relaxed, peaceful, and calm practice rather than a strained or difficult practice. Remember the mind–breath connection: as long as the mind is calm, so is the breathing; as long as the breathing is calm, then so is the mind.

SOUNDING THE AUM

This exercise can be practiced using the Meditation CD.

1. Seat yourself comfortably either in a chair or sitting on a cushion on the floor cross-legged or in the Lotus or Half Lotus..

2. Close your eyes and focus on a steady, relaxed, and regular breathing pattern. Breathe through the nose only.

3. If you are inexperienced, begin with a simple humming sound and feel the hum "buzz" in the roof of the mouth and vibrate in the head. The hum is regular and tuneless.

4. Begin the AUM from the navel, just under the diaphragm at the base of the lower ribs.

5. Begin by taking an in-breath, and, with mouth open, draw the AUM up from the navel. The AUM resonates up into the throat and larynx and is directed to the upper palate. The AUM then vibrates upward from here into the head. AUM ends with the closing of the lips, completed by a humming sound. Feel the energy of AUM diffusing and vibrating throughout the head.

6. Take another breath and begin again.

7. Try at least 10 rounds of AUM. Do more if you feel capable.

8. Remember the sound should be a steady hum, not a tune. Listen to my voice on the CD as a guide.

THE COMPONENTS OF AUM

AUM begins with sounding "AU" (as in audition). The whole of this sound is carried up through the body as outlined earlier as a long, drawn-out, and powerful intonation. As the mouth closes, the "M" of the mantra vibrates on the lips in a hum, and the hum vibrates up into the head. The breath expends itself prior to taking the next in-breath.

THE CHAKRAS

The chakras, which we spoke of in chapter 6, are an excellent focus for the mind, the breath and the energy of prana. It is excellent to sound the AUM in the chakras. By sounding AUM here, you will purify many negative states and will, over a period of time, feel uplifted as a result. Let us remind ourselves of how to do this.

AUM IN THE CHAKRAS

This exercise can be practiced using the Meditation CD.

1. Begin with a few rounds of digital pranayama.

2. Then do five minutes of candle gazing (optional).

3. Close the eyes and visualize a bright, golden light at the base of the Spine Chakra. Breathe steadily in and out through the nostrils while remaining mentally focused on the chakra. See the chakra begin to glow like a brilliant sun.

4. After some moments of breathing and visualizing at the chakra, resonate the AUM there. You may do this only once if you wish, or three times, or seven times in each chakra. Three and seven are mystical numbers but I don't think that the number of AUMs is necessarily as important as the quality of the sound. Aim for quality rather than quantity. However, keep the number of AUMs consistent for each chakra for the sake of discipline and an orderly mind.

5. Move up through all of the chakras in exactly the same manner.

6. When you reach the Crown Chakra, remain there for some time longer and visualize the concentration of bright light as much more powerful than in the other centers. See the light in the head radiating out for as far as you can.

AFTERWORD

Beyond all these techniques lies a great vista of spiritual experience. That is up to you to find. But the secret of finding what you seek lies within you. As Christ said, "The Kingdom of Heaven is within you."

So, as in our analogy of the caver, we have discovered the rich treasure that lies within the depths of the cave, and, discovering it, we return once again to the surface, bringing our treasure with us. No one else will understand what you have found unless that person has also entered the cave of the inner Self and has likewise undergone the journey within. But that really does not matter. Everyone finds his or her own pathway one way or another. In meditation you have dared to discover what matters most of all, and in that discovery you have found a freedom and peace that is beyond the things of this world.

By drinking from the well of the inner self you have become filled. You will only ever really find refreshment there. The world will not give you that. In meditation you have turned the key to your soul. You now know that you can always enter that place at will. Having turned the key, the door stands open leading to an inner sanctum. Go within, and may peace fill your mind and comfort your heart.

Stephen Austen, January 2002

FURTHER READING

Meditation and Mantras. *By Swami Vishnu Devananda.*
Published by Om Lotus Publishing Company, New York, or Sivananda Yoga Vedanta Centers worldwide.

How to Meditate. *By Lawrence LeShan Ph.D.*
Published by Bantam Books.

Letters on Occult Meditation. *By Alice A. Bailey.*
Published by Lucis Press Ltd. London, and Lucis Publishing Company, New York.

The Bhagavad Gita. *Translated by His Divine Grace A.C. Bhaktivedanta Swami Prabhupada.*
Published by The Bhaktivedanta Book Trust.

The Bible. (The New Testament in particular).

The Aquarian Gospel of Jesus The Christ. *By Levi.*
Published by L.N. Fowler & Co. Ltd. London.

The Light of the Soul. *By Alice A. Bailey.*
Published by Lucis Press Ltd. London.
Lucis Publishing Company, New York.

Science of Yoga series. *By Swami Sivananda.*
In particular in this series,
Volume 9, Raja Yoga
Volume 12, Science of Pranayama
Volume 17, Thought Power
Published by Sivananda Press.
Contact Sivananda Yoga Vedanta Centers worldwide.

Light on Pranayama. *By B.K.S. Iyengar.*
Published by Thorsons, HarperCollins, London.

The Case for Reincarnation. *By Joe Fisher.*
Published by Granada Books, London.

Functional Human Anatomy. *By James E. Crouch.*
Published by Lea & Febiger, Philadelphia.

Principles of Anatomy and Physiology. *By Gerard J. Tortora & Nicholas P. Anagnostakos.*
Published by HarperCollins, London.

ACKNOWLEDGMENTS & PICTURE CREDITS

My deeply grateful thanks to Debbie Thorpe of Godsfield Press, who had the vision to see this book in print, and without whom it would not have been possible. Thanks also to Jane Alexander, Joanne Jessop, Fiona Biggs, and especially Lizzy Gray and Lisa McCormick of Bridgewater Book Company, and all the publishing team that contributed to the book in both great and small ways.

The publisher's would like to thank the following for use of pictures:
CORBIS/STOCKMARKET: p.67; GETTYONESTONE: pp: 2, 12, 14L, 20, 27, 29, 36B, 41, 42, 63, 64, 74, 82, 83, 89, 104, 108; IMAGE BANK: pp: 4, 8B, 25, 31, 45L, 71, 77, 90, 103, 107, 112, 113, 114, 117, 118; NASA: p.43; TELEGRAPH COLOUR LIBRARY: pp: 10/11, 13, 34, 58, 61, 73, 78, 98.
COVER: Corbis/StockMarket.

INDEX

INDEX